RETAIL CRAP

Tales From the Front

Howard Harrison

Author of "*Corporate Crap: Lessons Learned From 40 Years in Corporate America*"

ISBN: 978-1-09839-986-3 (printed)
ISBN: 978-1-09839-987-0 (eBook)

Printed in the United States of America.

DEDICATION

I dedicate this book to all the people who work in retail. It is indeed a jungle out there. Hope you enjoy the narrative. All the best.

CONTENTS

Introduction ix

Chapter 1: The Pandemic... 1

Unsung Heroes

Chapter 2: Bankruptcies/Store Closings 5

Keeping the Doors Open

Chapter 3: Malls.. 11

Little Cities

Chapter 4: The Retail Workforce 15

Help Wanted

Chapter 5: Automation.. 19

Check This Out

Chapter 6: Online Shopping.. 26

Come on, people. Get off your naked asses!

Chapter 7: More Technology.. 32

Science Fiction and Big Brother

Chapter 8: Karen.. 37

"The Customer is Always Right!" (No, they're not.)

Chapter 9: Retail Crime... 42

Stopping the Steal

Chapter 10: Schemes and Scams 52

Many Happy Returns

Chapter 11: Babysitting 57

"Kids will be kids!"

Chapter 12: Attendance 62

No Call/No Show

Chapter 13: Holidays 68

Tis the Season

Chapter 14: Closing Time 74

Would you get the hell out of here already?

Chapter 15: My Store 77

How I would do things

INTRODUCTION

My total retail experience consists of three years as a part-time shipping clerk/stock boy for a women's clothing store while in high school from 1972 to 1974. Why in the world would I now want to write a book about the U.S. retail industry? Couple reasons.

First, like you, I am a customer. I buy things like everyone else. And whether you buy oranges at the supermarket or a bracelet online, you are a customer of some retailer. Some stores call us "guests" instead of customers for the same reason they call employees "associates" or "team members" instead of employees. It makes them feel better about themselves and they think it makes us feel better about ourselves. But retailers, employees, and customers do not spend much time singing Kumbaya together. The relationships are downright combative.

Whatever you call the combatants, the retail world is a battlefield. Customers want the best price and service. Employees want respect and a livable wage. Retailers want to make a buck. These things all clash. From the way retailers treat employees and customers to the way employees and customers treat retailers, it is a fascinating mix of commerce and human behavior.

The other thing that prompted me to write this book is that I am married to a Target "team leader." My wife comes home every day with stories of shoplifters, employees who don't show up, customers who insist on using expired coupons, and countless other "tales from the front."

"You should write a book," I'd tell her.

"No, you should," she'd tell me. "You're the writer."

She had a point. So I took her up on it.

Eileen has more than 40 years of experience in retail, from working the counter at Dairy Queen to serving as store manager for various retail chains. She provided much input and guidance as I researched the retail industry. I also talked to employees, store managers and others in retail, and culled stories from social media, where employees in retail routinely spout off with their own tales of woe.

I began working on this book before the COVID-19 pandemic, then put it on hold because of the impact the coronavirus was having on the retail industry. Whenever we get back to normal, I wonder if people will maintain a higher level of respect for those in retail who must deal with the American buying public.

Retail is a tough business. Competition is intense. Profit margins are slim. The Internet continues to threaten the continued existence of bricks and mortar. This book focuses mostly on the people who work in the stores. They are the ones who do the work. They are the ones who deal with what I call "retail crap."

This book is for them.

—— **CHAPTER** ——

1

Unsung Heroes

"Due to high demand and to support all guests, we will be limiting the quantities of toilet paper and flushable wipes to 1 per guest. We apologize for any inconvenience."

Signs like this appeared in stores across the United States in the early stages of the coronavirus pandemic of 2020. No, the coronavirus was not caused by having a dirty ass, but you would think it was given the run on toilet paper. We were told to stay home, and for some reason, people seemed to fear running out of toilet paper. We were told to stay home to stay safe. We were told it was a valley of death out there.

Not everyone was told to stay home. Health-care workers, firemen, police, and others who worked for "essential businesses" had to carry on despite the risks. Also told not told to stay home were retail workers, or at least those working in grocery stores, pharmacies and department stores that sold food and drugs along with hand sanitizers, antiseptic wipes, and of course, toilet paper.

Most workers at Costco, Walmart, Target, and other grocery and drug store chains make little more than minimum wage. Yet these people risked their lives and those of their loved ones to stock shelves, ring up groceries, and take unprecedented abuse from the buying public during the pandemic.

I was grateful that my wife, a Target store team leader, still had a job, as the coronavirus caused many people to lose theirs. But I worried if it was worth the risk.

"We had over 9,000 visitors in our store the day the stay-at-home order took effect," said one Walmart store manager. "I feel like my odds of winning the lottery are better than staying well."

Retail workers likened their situation to being in the band on the Titanic that kept playing while the ship was sinking. "All retail workers should be getting hazard pay," one said.

My wife has told me all about the abuse retail employees – or team members, associates, or whatever "Corporate" wants to call them – put up with every day. And this was *before* the pandemic.

"At the start of my shift, I spent 15 minutes arguing with a customer, telling him that I cannot take his $20 bill from the Bahamas," says one employee. "Then a woman's 'service dog' pug takes a crap in the middle of the store. Then a woman goes full Karen because I won't take a personal check for lottery tickets. I want to go home."

But the coronavirus brought out the worst in people. They started buying everything up like the world was ending. Then they berated the guy stacking potatoes because there was no toilet paper.

"I know you have more in the back," they snarl, as if every retailer not only has a "back" but that they're hiding merchandise there.

"There ain't no back," said one employee. "The back has an employee bathroom and a clipboard with a schedule on it."

"Can't you check the warehouse?" pleads another customer, as if there is a replenishment center down the road.

Retail workers must always deal with shoplifters who seem to believe they have a God-given right to take shit that doesn't belong to them and then are indignant when they're caught. But the coronavirus made things even uglier.

"At the supermarket where I work there is a plastic hand sanitizer dispenser on the wall. A guy walked up to it, broke it open, took the bag of sanitizer out and walked out with it. Unfortunately, I'd have gotten in trouble if I'd gone after the scumbag. But geez!"

The whole toilet paper thing was particularly ugly. Fistfights in the aisles over toilet paper. Customers mugged in parking lots over toilet paper.

"People broke in through the back door to get toilet paper. A customer was telling people to go around back, that we were stashing toilet paper back there. There was almost a riot."

Customers lucky enough to get toilet paper had legitimate fear of getting mugged in the parking lot for it.

"I bought two 18-packs of toilet paper at Walmart," said one customer. "The cashier asked me if I wanted help out to my car. I said I could handle it. In retrospect, I think it was probably for the protection of myself and my daughter."

"I am carrying mace daily," said one retail worker. "I don't know if I will ever be able to see people the same way again."

"If it was up to me, I would just toss a pallet of toilet paper into the parking lot and let the animals maul themselves over it," said another.

The coronavirus closed schools, so naturally parents let the kids run loose in their favorite retail establishments.

"What is the point of closing all the schools, libraries, and restaurants if the kids are just hanging out at the stores with their friends, bouncing basketballs, riding scooters in the aisles, laughing, and knocking stuff over?" my wife lamented.

Hey, parents out there: I know your kids are off from school. But turning them loose at the nearest Target to fill their time is plain irresponsible, both during and not during a global pandemic.

Online ordering, curbside pickup and "contactless" delivery became the rage. I could not understand "contactless." What do they do, throw it at you?

The pandemic did do one positive thing for retail workers, however. It led some people to call them "unsung heroes" for the role they played in keeping us all fed, clothed, and stocked with the essentials we need to live. Maybe now their pay will increase or they will be treated with more respect. Or maybe not.

—— CHAPTER ——

2

Keeping the Doors Open

When the first Toys R Us opened in Chicago's northwest suburbs in the 1960s, tales of its size and scale reached my neighborhood and took on mythical proportions. Nothing was more magical to a kid than a toy store, and this one, it was said, was gigantic and wall-to-wall toys.

Before Toys R Us, the only toy stores I had known were small, local toy stores. The big department stores had toy departments, but I never heard of a store so big that was *all toys!* Later, Toys R Us held the same fascination for my own kids.

Now it is gone. So are Blockbuster Video, Tower Records, Borders, and other stores where you could browse for toys, books, music, movies, and other sensory items for hours. The visceral satisfaction of browsing live for merchandise, of seeing and touching what you may want to buy versus pressing buttons on a phone or computer, is something fewer people seem to value.

Shopping is something many people love to do, and at the very least, something most people must do to get what they need. Global retail sales are estimated to total close to $30 *trillion.* Yet, despite this huge pie, many retailers today – especially those that rely on foot traffic – are having a hard time staying open.

Dozens of chains, from Macy's to Victoria's Secret to Party City, have closed hundreds of locations. Others, like Payless ShoeSource, Circuit City, and Pier 1 Imports, have vanished completely. Analysts say there are too many physical stores in the U.S. given the popularity of online shopping – and this was before the COVID-19 lockdown had people feeling skittish about venturing out.

Department stores have been particularly affected. In the 1980s, department stores accounted for about 10 percent of retail sales. Today it is barely over 1 percent, and that includes online sales. Sears, J.C. Penney, and Neiman Marcus are among those to file for Chapter 11 bankruptcy protection.

Some of us grew up when Sears, Roebuck and Company was the preeminent department store chain in America. Founded in 1893 as a mail-order catalog company, Sears opened its first retail store in Evansville, Indiana, in 1925. For the next 64 years, Sears generated more revenue than any other retailer in the United States. Not until 1989 did Walmart surpass Sears in annual revenue.

By October 2018, when Sears filed for bankruptcy, the company was just the 31st largest U.S. retailer. It had 687 Sears and Kmart stores (Kmart had acquired Sears in 2005 to form Sears Holdings), down from 1,672 stores in January 2016. Hundreds more stores closed in 2019. Years of declining sales led to all this. Sears Holdings had lost more than $11 billion since 2011.

Then came 2020. As if retailers were not suffering enough, the pandemic dealt a death blow to many. Clothing retailers could no longer allow shoppers to try on clothes. Lord & Taylor, J. Crew, Brooks Brothers, Barneys New York, and Tailored Brands (parent company of Men's Warehouse and Jos. A Banks) all filed for bankruptcy protection in 2020. Victoria's Secret closed more than 200 stores in 2020 and was still closing more in 2021.

In all, a record 12,200 U.S. stores closed in 2020, about 2,000 more than in 2019. There were also a record number of bankruptcies – 603, including 125 retail and consumer goods firms. The pandemic forced stores not deemed "essential businesses" to close for most of the spring and into the summer, driving even more shoppers online.

Of course, there were some winners. Retailers like Costco, Target, and Walmart, and drug store chains like Walgreens and CVS, were deemed essential businesses because they sold food and other items essential to one's everyday living. This gave them an advantage over stores like Kohl's, Nordstrom, and Macy's.

Macy's, for example, announced plans to close an additional 125 stores over the next three years and cut 2,000 corporate jobs as it attempts to reinvent itself due to sagging sales. Target, on the other hand, grew its 2020 sales by more than $15 billion over prior year – greater than the company's total sales growth over the previous 11 years. Two-thirds of the growth was from digital sales, which grew 145 percent, driven by 235 percent growth in same-day services (order pick-up, drive-up and direct ship). Drive-up led the way with growth of more than 500 percent over prior year. The company gained about $9 billion in market share.

Given Target's strong performance and Macy's struggles, you would think the people in Chicago's "Gold Coast" neighborhood would be thrilled to have Target replace the Macy's that was closing in Water Tower Place, a nine-story vertical mall on the city's "Magnificent Mile." But you would be wrong.

The Magnificent Mile is a section of Michigan Avenue in downtown Chicago that runs from the Chicago River to Oak Street in a neighborhood called "The Gold Coast." The moniker reflects the neighborhood's proximity to the shores of Lake Michigan and its many upscale restaurants, hotels, and shops.

One of the most prominent locations on the Mag Mile was the Macy's store at Michigan and Oak. It was the corner hub of Water Tower Place, so named because the mall is across the street from a water tower that was one of the only things to survive the Great Chicago Fire of 1871.

Water Tower Place is a popular tourist attraction. Macy's occupied space on all nine floors.

In January 2021, Macy's announced it was closing the Water Tower store. The closure created the largest available retail space in Chicago: 323,812 square feet, including 227,212 square feet of selling space, up and down the nine floors. A leading contender to fill the space was Target, which was investing $4 billion in expansion initiatives in 2021, including 40 new stores and 150 remodels.

The reason Gold Coast residents weren't happy about replacing a struggling business with a thriving one – particularly one that sells things we all need and use every day – is because many of the people who live in the Gold Coast are wealthy and snobby and felt it was a step down in class.

"How embarrassing is this to the city?" exclaimed Cook County Treasurer Maria Pappas, who lives in the neighborhood. "I'm trying to figure out what is magnificent on the Magnificent Mile about Target. It's disgusting. You don't put Target next to Gucci, Louis Vuitton and everything else on Oak Street. It demeans the quality of Michigan Avenue."

When challenged that this seemed like an elitist attitude, Pappas doubled down.

"There's nothing elitist about this. This is simply saying, 'Please don't sell celery and carrots in Water Tower.' It's a magnificent structure."

Heidi Stevens, a columnist at the *Chicago Tribune*, wrote that unlike Pappas, she thought it was great for a store with affordable merchandise to anchor Water Tower Place.

"I love the idea of families making a pilgrimage to the American Girl Doll store, maybe shelling out the money for a doll, then ducking next door to buy eight doll outfits for the price of one tiny AG tutu. I love the idea of all that square footage being filled with stuff that's useful (school supplies, laundry detergent, groceries) and affordable (throw pillows that cost $22 instead of $200). What's embarrassing about an affordable store among a sea of high-end retailers? Do $19 handbags upset the moral order? Is there something off-putting, a little *déclassé* about folks who wear $14 Target leggings mingling with folks who pay $98 at nearby Lululemon?"

In addition to being elitist, Pappas's concerns seem irrational given that other Michigan Avenue neighbors include a Walgreens, Starbucks, Disney Store, Cheesecake Factory, and even discount retailers like T.J. Maxx and Marshalls. Water Tower Place has a food court that sells greasier fare than celery and carrots. And is Macy's really that high-end?

The fact is, Target has its shit together while other retail chains like Macy's have either gone out of business or are struggling to reinvent themselves. I guess to some people in the neighborhood, a store like Target that would create more jobs, pay more taxes, and generate more revenue than Macy's is not worth the blow to their ego. But they're okay with Cheesecake Factory. Go figure.

As this book went to press, it was reported that Target was no longer considering replacing Macy's in Water Tower Place.

"This is pure speculation, but I believe negative publicity was a factor," said Chicago alderman Brian Hopkins, whose ward includes the Water Tower location. "I don't enjoy seeing a space as large as the Macy's space languishing."

And languish it did. The space, which had never been vacant since the mall opened in 1975, remained vacant for most of 2021 as Brookfield Properties, the mall owner, continued to search for a suitable tenant. Brookfield was also struggling to fill other vacancies in the mall, particularly on the upper floors, which are harder to fill even in good economic times. And, they were competing with numerous storefronts along Michigan Avenue that had closed. A survey conducted in April 2021 found 28 vacant storefronts, representing more than 25 percent of the 110 businesses on the Mag Mile.

In the *Chicago Tribune* "Letters to the Editor" column, one reader had this to say:

"Cook County Treasurer Maria Pappas' comment on Target being an 'embarrassment' to the Mag Mile was a slap in the face to a company that has already invested in Chicago. I am hardly surprised it walked because of not just that but also the elevated city violence, which has made its way downtown. Shunning a growth and income generator because of a snobby attitude is just wrong. Good luck renting a space that large in today's environment. The stupidity of local politicians never ceases to amaze me."

In the meantime, Target continues to thrive. The company gave $500 bonuses to all hourly workers and $1,000 to $2,000 bonuses to store managers and others in leadership roles in 2020 while raising its starting pay to $15 an hour. The company provided another round of bonuses in 2021. In 2022, Target will upgrade 200 more stores and continue to invest in new technologies to support the company's fast-growing e-commerce business. The company also is partnering with Ulta Beauty to open scaled-down Ulta Beauty shops in as many as 800 Target stores.

"We saw record growth in 2020 as our guests turned to Target to safely provide for their families throughout the pandemic," said Target Chairman and Chief Executive Officer Brian Cornell. "As we look ahead to 2021 and beyond, we see continued opportunity to invest."

Just not in Water Tower Place.

—— **CHAPTER** ——

3

Little Cities

In September 1971, Woodfield Mall opened in Schaumburg, Illinois, a suburb of Chicago about 30 miles west of the city. With 59 stores, it was the largest shopping mall in the United States. More amazing, all the stores were under one roof. It made Woodfield seem like the eighth wonder of the world to me. Woodfield was not the first enclosed mall. That was the Southdale Center in Edina, Minnesota, which opened in 1956. But it was the first "mega" indoor mall.

I was starting my sophomore year of high school, just a few months shy of turning 16. Soon I would get my driver's license and buy my first car: a 1967 fire-engine red Mustang for $900. I had a part-time job as a shipping clerk/stock boy for Best & Co., a women's clothing store in the Old Orchard Shopping Center across the street from my high school. I was making $1.65 an hour, minimum wage at the time. Gas was about 30 cents a gallon.

Old Orchard was an outdoor mall with a Marshall Field's, Montgomery Wards and at least a couple dozen other stores. It was one of the largest shopping centers in Chicago. I couldn't imagine one even larger all under one roof. As soon as I got my driver's license, I had to go see Woodfield.

The idea that I'd choose a shopping mall as one of my first destinations upon getting my driver's license is even more laughable when you consider that I abhor shopping even more than most Cro-Magnon men of my generation. What I remember most vividly about Woodfield is the Hot Sam Pretzels. I don't think I'd ever had a hot pretzel before. I also remember seeing the big orange Woodfield water tower out in the distance as I started getting close. That was the big identifier. Back then Schaumburg was kind of out in the sticks. Today it's so built up you can't even see the water tower anymore on approach.

Woodfield was named after General Robert E. Wood, former chairman of Sears, and Marshall Field, founder of Marshall Field and Company. Sears and Marshall Field's were two of Woodfield's flagship stores.

Today, despite having grown to nearly 250 stores and restaurants, Woodfield is no longer close to being the largest shopping mall in the United States. It's ranked no higher than 12th although it is still the largest mall in the Chicago area and remains a popular tourist attraction.

Indoor malls like Woodfield proliferated in the 1980s, mostly in suburban locations. Today, there are Woodfield clones in or near seemingly every community. The largest mall in the United States is the Mall of America in Bloomington, Minnesota. The largest in North America is West Edmonton Mall in Alberta, Canada. The world's four largest malls are all in China.

The shopping mall – indoor or outdoor – is a modern version of the historical town marketplace. In his 1985 book "*The Malling of America*, William Kowinski called malls "the new Main Streets of America." The mall became a place for seniors in warm-up suits to walk the mall's corridors before most stores even opened to get their morning exercise. It became a gathering place for teenagers to hang out, work their first jobs, and find romance.

"Some people work more than one store," says one mall employee. "You might have part-time hours at one store and part-time hours at another, which creates a larger social circle. So when you're doing your Friday night out after work at Applebee's, Fridays, Chili's or whatever restaurant/bar in the mall is your preferred after-hours hangout, you'll have people not just from your store but from other stores where people from your store work."

Many mall employees met their spouses at the mall. Had I worked at a mall after college, I'm sure I would have. Almost all of my social relationships after college were with or through people I worked with.

"There are so many ways to meet people," says another mall employee. "There might be a cute girl at One Potato, Two Potato or Sbarro's and you can go by at lunch. Or your friend knows someone who works at Limited so you go out with all the Limited girls. Or at any bar in the mall, it gives you something to talk about. 'Oh, you work at Limited, don't you? I work at Abercrombie.'"

"When I worked at Payless Shoes, our back room was adjacent to the back room of Susie's Casuals," says a male employee. "Almost all of my fellow co-workers were men and we would flirt regularly with the Susie's Casuals girls."

Today, many malls are closing due to online shopping and other market forces described earlier. The pandemic also crushed mall traffic. Anchor stores like Sears and Macy's are going away. Even mainstays like Spencer Gifts, Sunglass Hut and Hallmark Cards are disappearing from a growing number of malls. Up to 25 percent of U.S. malls are expected to close in the next five years.

Other malls are transforming themselves into business, entertainment, and residential complexes, taking the "town marketplace" concept even further. They are becoming little cities. Instead of Macy's, there might be a grocery store, comedy club, gym, or apartment building among a diverse array of retail establishments.

"Top-tier malls still have no problem attracting shoppers," says Mary Brett Whitfield, senior vice president, Kantar Retail. "These malls are most likely to have a combination of entertainment, restaurant, and retail options that deliver a compelling experience, something that is more engaging than the ease of shopping online."

Retailers are trying to appeal to younger people as much as possible. A larger percentage of Millennials (62%) say they "love/enjoy shopping," compared with Gen X (54%) and Boomers (40%), according to data from *Lifestyle Monitor*. So, the idea is to give them more shopping experience to enjoy.

A spokeswoman for the International Council of Shopping Centers in New York says malls will continue to evolve with "a rise in non-apparel tenants." Among the more novel are what she calls "experiential offerings" and "competitive socializing." This includes things like golf, ax-throwing, and escape rooms.

As mixed-use retail/residential communities continue to take root, malls become even more like little cities. "Not all of them will have water parks, amusement rides or mini golf," she says. "But the options of what they may contain is limitless."

CHAPTER

4

Help Wanted

On the Facebook page *Retail Life*, a store manager reported that she hired a new employee on Friday, asked him if he could start on Monday, he said yes, then he failed to show up. On Tuesday, the store manager received a text from the guy saying his grandmother broke her hip, he has been out of town, but he's home now and could come in tomorrow (Wednesday) if she still wanted him.

"I'm all for second chances so I said fine and told him to come in Wednesday," she said. Then he failed to show up on Wednesday. "This time his excuse was he thought I said Thursday."

Remarkably, this manager was asking on Facebook if she should give this guy yet another chance. "I have two more people wanting the job," she said.

I would have sent him packing after the "grandma-broke-her-hip" story. Even if it were true, if I were supposed to start a new job that day, I would find the time to call my employer to let them know why I could not make it. I would not wait until the next day to send a text message.

The fact this store manager was still considering hiring this guy shows how hard it is to find reliable employees in retail. As you will read in the chapter on attendance, the "no call/no show" is remarkably common among retail workers. In the example above, this guy had not even started and he had this down.

I believe one reason many retail workers do not take their jobs as seriously as they should is because they are lower paid than the rest of the U.S. workforce, according to the U.S. Census Bureau. For what it is worth, they are also younger, less educated, and more female. A slightly larger percentage of minorities work in retail than in other industries, although non-Hispanic Whites still make up 60 percent of the U.S. retail workforce.

More than half of retail workers are between 16 and 34 years old. More than 55 percent are women. Blacks comprise about 12 percent of the retail workforce, Hispanics about 19 percent. About 18 percent of retail workers have college degrees compared to 35 percent of the total U.S. workforce.

More than 10 million people work today as cashiers, retail salespersons, or first-line supervisors of retail salespersons, accounting for more than 6 percent of the U.S. labor force. More than a million retail workers work in grocery stores. Close to another million work in general merchandise stores, including warehouse clubs and supercenters. More than a half-million work in department stores.

Cashiers are among the lowest-paid retail employees. (At Target, cashiers are called "guest advocates." Target really takes the whole "guest" thing to an extreme.) Regular full-time cashiers make an average of about $22,000 a year. Retail salespersons average about $35,000. First-line supervisors of retail salespeople average $42,000. The median earnings for regular full-time workers in the total workforce is close to $50,000.

One consequence of all the bankruptcies and store closings in the retail industry is that a lot of employees lost their jobs. This was exacerbated by the forced closings and lost business caused by COVID-19 at businesses other than retailers like Target, Walmart, and Kroger, which added employees during the pandemic. And, of course, growth in online sales have reduced the need for on-site employees.

As the pandemic lifted in 2021 and people began to venture out again, much was made of staffing shortages and difficulty in hiring people at many retail establishments. Some people believed that increased unemployment benefits and pandemic-related stimulus payments had reduced the incentive people had to work. Most economists were skeptical of this. They instead point to the low pay and poor working conditions in most retail jobs, with retail wages making it difficult for a person to maintain even the most basic standards of living.

Economists at the Massachusetts Institute of Technology, for example, looked at what a person living in St. Louis would need to cover essential expenses. They came up with a minimum of $14 an hour if you were single and $21 an hour if you had one child. The owner of three Express franchises in St. Louis says it is hard to find people who will work for less than $14 an hour. She says part of the problem is that employers in the retail industry have gotten used to the low pay and the ability to dictate schedules and other conditions.

"A labor shortage is not going on here," says Sylvia Allegretto, labor economist and co-chair of the Center on Wage and Employment Dynamics at the University of California-Berkeley. "No one is asking these businesses if they tried to offer better pay or benefits. These jobs in retail and restaurants are some of the lowest-paid and lowest job quality. If people are not accepting these jobs, employers should think about increasing the attractiveness of the job."

The biggest argument against raising people's wages is that it would result in fewer jobs. "A higher minimum wage does not benefit the workers it causes to be unemployed," says Joe Barnett, a research fellow with the Heartland Institute. "A minimum wage hike is like a penalty for employing low-skilled employees. In effect, it cuts off a couple of lower rungs on the ladder of employment opportunities for young, inexperienced workers."

I am more skeptical of the cause-and-effect of raising the minimum wage. The minimum wage itself is already arbitrary. If it were raised, I believe the market would adjust. If there would be fewer jobs but the ones remaining had better paid and therefore more dedicated employees, is that necessarily a bad thing? And if the jobs that are eliminated can be eliminated so easily, how important were these jobs to begin with? Or maybe the CEOs of the big retail chains might want to consider reducing their own $20 million annual compensation packages?

I am not necessarily endorsing a higher minimum wage. I'm just skeptical of all the studies that *project* the job losses that would result *if* a higher minimum wage were instituted. And even if a higher minimum wage does cost jobs, is this a reason not to raise it? What's better, a lot of low-paying jobs and low employee satisfaction or fewer but better paying jobs that employees will take more seriously and that allow them to support themselves and their families? How about we start with a wage that would allow a person working 40 hours a week to exist without welfare and from there let the market decide?

Bank of America Chairman and CEO Brian Moynihan apparently agrees with me. He recently announced that Bank of America was raising the minimum wage for its employees to $20 an hour. "If you get a job at Bank of America, you'll make $41,000 a year," Moynihan said.

Whether they implement a higher minimum wage or not, most businesses are trying to find ways to operate with fewer people, and they would do this whether there was a labor shortage or not. Businesses do not exist to provide jobs. They exist to make money. If they can get the customer's money without having to pay a cashier, they will. Self-checkout, self-serve kiosks, "cashless" stores and other forms of automation are supposed to improve efficiency. The fact is, they are designed to put retail employees out of work.

CHAPTER

5

Check This Out

I am not a people person. I am also not a technology person. This makes me a conflicted person when it comes to self-checkout.

As an introvert, I like not dealing with a human. But self-checkout, especially at the grocery store, is a pain.

- You have to weigh most of the fruits and vegetables.

- If a barcode is missing, you have to find the specific fruit or vegetable in the touchscreen's data base, which is not easy when there are 12 different kinds of apples.

- There is always some item that doesn't have a bar code, or it's wrinkled and can't be read.

- Some items are banned from self-checkout, like alcohol, but most people don't know that so you try to put it through anyway and someone has to come fix the mess you just created.

- You must make sure to put the item in the right place after you scan it.

- You have to do your own bagging.

All in all, I find it much easier and faster to use a cashier.

Of course, the motive behind self-checkout is not efficiency as much as not having to pay a cashier. Yet, in any retail store that has self-check-out, you need people to supervise the self-checkout, so does this not defeat the purpose?

There will always be customers who have trouble at self-checkout. Customers often leave stuff behind at self-checkout because there is no cashier or bagger to say, "Excuse me, sir, you forgot this." There are people who get in the self-checkout lane without realizing it is the self-checkout lane or that don't have enough money so they have to call someone over to take stuff out of their basket.

"Then the customers waiting behind them get pissed because this dufus filled his whole basket before realizing he only has $6," says one employee.

Then there is the problem of using self-checkout on items that have sensors, like clothing. The customer can't take these things off. A store employee has to come over and take them off. Many customers are impatient and try to leave the store with them on, setting off the alarm.

To me, this is the epitome of inefficiency. You should not be able to use self-checkout if you are purchasing items with sensors, and there should be a big sign at stores like Walmart and Target that say that. Instead, there has to be a person manning self-checkout that notices the sensors and says, "Sir, after you finish your transaction, I have to take those sensors off before you leave."

Retailers claim self-checkout "frees up" employees for more valuable tasks. But if self-checkout creates all these other needs, is it worth it?

"What I find aggravating is that customers choose self-checkout of their own free will – we don't force anyone to use the self-checkout – but then they complain the whole time they're at self-checkout," says another employee. "Even when there are full-service lanes open, they go to self-checkout and then complain the whole time. Hey, you didn't have to use self-checkout."

Self-checkout got a shot in the arm when COVID-19 made some people skittish about interacting with other human beings and those human beings touching their groceries. But until they work the bugs out of these systems, the self-checkout supervisor job seems safe.

"The lesson of self-checkout," says Lisa Kresge, research and policy expert at the University of California-Berkeley Center for Labor Research and Education, "is that all this technology still requires a substantial amount of human labor to back up these systems."

Ariel Shemesh, CEO of a company called KanduAI, invented artificial intelligence-based software to enhance self-checkout systems in grocery stores. "Most shoppers want to use self-checkout but because of the sometimes-complex user experience they avoid using it," he says. "The best thing you can do to entice your shoppers to use the self-checkout is to make it super simple and intuitive to use."

The KanduAI technology addresses the problem of having to look up your produce and other non-barcoded items on the touchscreen through what Shemesh calls "computer vision, which recognizes the item placed on the scanner."

In the future, Shemesh sees "scan-and-go carts" being used, particularly for express lanes of 10 items or less, and "self-checkout counters without a need for barcode scanning. The entire checkout will be done through AI cameras."

In other words, a customer can take a product off the shelf, put it in their cart, and no one touches it again till they put everything in their car. Computer vision enables the whole cart to be scanned at once. "Once the loss-prevention pieces get ironed out," Shemesh says.

According to people I talked to who work in stores with self-checkout, the self-checkout lanes are often used by thieves. "It's easier to sneak things through," one says. "One person supervising self-checkout can't watch every transaction."

Another technology growing in popularity is the self-serve kiosk. My first experiences with these were at the airport. Instead of waiting in line to give your ticket to an agent who would then hand you your boarding pass and check your luggage, you wait in line for a kiosk. At the kiosk, you punch in your flight details, personal identification and other information and it spits out your boarding pass and luggage tags. Then you wait in another line for an agent to check your bags.

There still must be agents on hand to direct passengers to the kiosks, assist people having trouble at the kiosks, tell people where to check their bags, and there still must be people at the baggage check-in stations. Like self-checkout, this does not seem to improve efficiency as much as provide a means to employ fewer people, even if it makes the process more difficult and stressful for customers.

McDonald's has implemented self-ordering kiosks at many of its locations. The person who monitors them is called a "guest experience leader." When my wife and I stopped at a McDonald's on our last road trip, this woman greeted us as we walked in and instructed us to use the kiosk to place our order even though the lines at the counter were not long. I don't recall the details but after multiple attempts to place our order via the kiosk, the guest experience leader finally had to come over and do it for us. It took us at least three times longer to order than if we had ordered at the counter.

But that's not the worst. The worst is that in one study, every McDonald's touchscreen examined tested positive for fecal bacteria. The study was conducted in England. Investigators swabbed the new self-order kiosk screens at six McDonald's locations. All came up positive.

"We were all surprised how much gut and (fecal) bacteria there was on the touchscreen machines," said Dr. Paul Matawele, senior lecturer in microbiology at London Metropolitan University. "These cause the kind of infections that people pick up in hospitals." The bacteria included staphylococcus, which has been linked to Toxic Shock Syndrome.

In response, a McDonald's representative said that "our self-order screens are cleaned frequently throughout the day. All of our restaurants also provide facilities for customers to wash their hands before eating."

Those facilities are probably where customers are picking up the fecal bacteria to begin with and we know not everyone washes their hands, so this is gross. Think about that next time you use a kiosk to order your Quarter Pounder w/Cheese.

In states where marijuana is legal, self-serve kiosks are being used in dispensaries. The kiosks display the menu of goodies available, allowing customers to order what they want without having to discuss it with anyone. They then simply pay an attendant at checkout. This is particularly convenient for regular customers who know what they want and don't need a consultation.

Speaking of convenient, where I live in southern California, you can order pot online and have it delivered to your door inside of an hour. You don't even have to go to a dispensary. It is easier than ordering a pizza.

Stores also are going "cashless." Customers who lick their fingers to separate each bill from a wad of cash before handing you each moistened bill one at a time will not be missed. But other than that, the move to cashless stores does not do cashiers any more favors than self-checkout.

Amazon has more than two dozen cashless supermarkets in the United States and in 2021 opened the first one outside the country in London. Shoppers use an app on their phone to scan a code that allows them to enter the store. Cameras and sensors then track what customers take off the shelves and put in their carts. The customer leaves without having to check out. The purchase automatically gets charged to their Amazon account and a receipt is sent to their email.

Some Hudson airport convenience stores have adopted the Amazon technology to create Hudson Nonstop cashier-less stores. Like the Amazon Go stores, Hudson shoppers swipe a credit card to enter, items are tracked by cameras and sensors, and they are billed automatically when they walk out instead of stopping at a cash register. Of course, here too, there must be Hudson employees on hand to brief customers on the process and answer questions. Hudson says convenience, not reducing headcount, is the primary aim.

For a business like an airport convenience store, not making a customer wait in line for a cash register can be the difference between making a sale or losing one if a rushed traveler does not have time to wait. But this benefit seems limited to a business like Hudson's. At the local 7-11, where people usually are not rushing to make a plane, I don't know that it would matter as much. And no matter how convenient or inconvenient, some customers will always still prefer a cashier.

There has been a backlash against cashless stores that has led several cities and states to ban them, including forcing Amazon to change its policy and agree to accept cash at its cashless stores. The criticism is not on behalf of retail cashiers but because cashless stores discriminate against people who do not have bank accounts, credit or debit cards, or smartphones.

One class of such individuals is homeless people. Many of the homeless people that hang around the Target where my wife works come in and steal stuff. But for other low-income people or anyone else who either must or would rather use cash to buy things, the cashless concept does indeed discriminate against them.

There are good reasons to go cashless. Most people born after the Baby Boomers almost never use cash. Going cashless can dissuade robbers and burglars. It can reduce other forms of loss, such as employee theft and bookkeeping errors. It can make transactions faster and more efficient. It can free up cashiers for other tasks. When you add the hygienic aspect, what is not to like?

"The potential societal cost of a cashless economy I think outweighs the potential benefits for business," says Ritchie Torres, a New York City councilman who proposed a statewide ban on cashless stores.

There is no federal law requiring businesses to accept cash, so states and cities are enacting their own laws. Massachusetts has a law that specifically prohibits discrimination against people who prefer to use cash. In 2019, New Jersey passed a law banning certain types of cashless stores, and Philadelphia became the first city to ban all cashless stores. Chicago, San Francisco, and Washington D.C. are among other cities considering such proposals.

While none of this enhances the future job prospects of cashiers, labor experts do not cite retail workers among the 25 professions most threatened by automation. The variables of human behavior and standards of customer satisfaction that are at the heart of the retail shopping experience will continue to require humans to navigate for the foreseeable future, it seems.

But not if retailers can help it.

—— CHAPTER ——

6

Come on, people. Get off your naked asses!

When I was growing up in the 1960s, the stereotype of the future was of machines taking over most everyday tasks while Man's legs and arms atrophied from inactivity. The way things are going, folks, this may not be far from the truth.

Before the coronavirus gave people a good excuse to have stuff delivered instead of getting off their asses to go to the store, the trend was already in place. One cannot argue the convenience of online ordering and home delivery. If my wife wants a particular type of sweater for Christmas, it is easier for me to find it online than search through stores. Of course, I never liked to shop to begin with.

Online shopping is a 21st century phenomenon, but department stores delivered merchandise to customers' homes via their own fleets of horse-drawn wagons as early as the 1800s. Of course, there wasn't a mall in every town back then and not everyone had their own horse.

Today in the Internet world, Amazon is king when it comes to online shopping. But Walmart, Target and other retailers have implemented their own online shopping and next-day or even same-day delivery services to keep up with Americans' penchant for convenience.

Retailers can offer next-day delivery of far more merchandise online than they can in stores. In 2020, Walmart offered next-day delivery of more than 220,000 items – about twice as many items as it carries in its stores – to more than 75 percent of the country. In 2021, it added thousands more items to its menu.

Curbside pickup soared in 2020 due to COVID-19. And like other consumer behaviors triggered by the pandemic, the desire to get your products without having to leave your car continues to grow.

"Order pickup has increased 600 percent from last year," says the order-fulfillment lead at a Target in suburban Chicago. "We are continually understaffed because the forecasts on which our staffing levels are based can't keep up. You end up having to pull both people and product from all other areas of the store, which then negatively affects those areas. It's a challenge."

Employees who put together online orders at Target, Walmart and similar retailers often play a game called "What Were They Thinking?" in which they speculate on the thought process or set of circumstances behind a particularly eclectic array of items.

"Like a bag of Cheetos, a laxative and Chapstick," says one order-fulfillment employee. "These three items they have to order online? What were they thinking? Come Valentine's Day, there is always a sharp increase in orders for vibrators. Or the hormonal woman ordering 12 boxes of tampons, four boxes of pads and a giant Hershey bar."

Retailers are pushing hard to improve their customer service when it comes to online orders and curbside delivery. If the process is too confusing, or they don't have enough curbside-pickup space, or they leave the customer waiting too long, or Heaven forbid the customer has to get off their ass and exit their car, there will be Hell to pay. If it was me, for the customer who ordered the bag of Cheetos, laxative and Chapstick, I'd let 'em wait.

Online ordering and delivery of groceries has become huge. I do most of the grocery shopping in our house and I do not like to order groceries online. I like to choose my own meat, fruit, and vegetables. I pay attention to expiration dates. And unlike my wife's sweater, I know what I want, I know where to find it, and grocery stores are very accessible where I live.

When you use Instacart, you are at the mercy of someone trying to get as many shopping trips done in the shortest amount of time. I used them once in the early days of the pandemic. When the guy substituted frozen salmon filets for fresh, that was the end of that for me.

But different strokes for different folks, I guess, given the popularity of Instacart and other grocery delivery services. Instacart employs more than 12,000 in-store shoppers and works with more than 130,000 independent contractors who shop for customers and deliver their groceries. The company was growing fast before the pandemic. The value of the online grocery market more than doubled from $12 billion in 2016 to $26 billion in 2018. Today, more than 10 percent of U.S. consumers say they buy their groceries online.

For people so busy they not only can't go to the store to get their own groceries, they don't have time to cook even if the groceries are delivered, meal delivery is the answer. This business also was growing fast before the pandemic but was abetted further by COVID-19. When restaurants were closed to indoor dining, Grubhub, Uber Eats and DoorDash couldn't deliver meals fast enough to the growing throngs of Americans who now had another reason to sit on their ass and eat greasy, sodium-laden prepared food out of Styrofoam containers.

All in all, the pandemic increased people's familiarity and comfort level with online shopping to the point where most American adults in a recent survey said they expect to split their shopping evenly between online and in-person in 2022. Pre-pandemic, 60 percent of adults said they shopped mostly in person. Today, only 37 percent say they shop mostly in person.

Doing your shopping from the privacy of your own home also allows you to shop naked, drunk, stoned, or whatever condition you happen to be in. It is estimated that Americans make more than $45 billion worth of drunken online purchases a year. In a survey on this subject, more than a quarter of respondents said they had made a drunken purchase within the last year. I don't know who thinks up these studies, but it also found:

- $444 is the average spend per drunk shopper.
- Clothing and shoes are the most common drunk purchases, followed by movies, games, and tech.
- Amazon is the preferred platform of drunken shoppers, with 85 percent of drunken shoppers surveyed calling Amazon their No.1 choice.

The average respondent in the survey was 36 years old with an income of $92,000 a year, more than twice the national average. Indeed, the higher the income, the more respondents reported making a drunk purchase. Women were slightly more likely than men to drunk shop (80% to 78%), although men spend more. The alcohol of choice is split between hard liquor (37%), beer (34%), and wine (29%). Men prefer beer (45%) and women wine (50%).

Most respondents said online shopping increases drunk impulse purchases, and 94 percent said they usually end up regretting their purchase. Eighty percent said they usually end up returning their purchase.

Of course, you don't have to shop online to shop drunk. Many people drunk shop in stores. One store employee told me of a woman who bought six 4-packs of Sutter Home and drank most of them before she reached the register. "At least she paid for them all."

"At the charity shop I worked we had a customer who was so drunk she urinated *and* defecated in the changing room – while wearing a pair of our jeans."

But back to online shopping. Yes, it is convenient, and the pool of goods to choose from is vast and can't be replicated in any bricks-and-mortar store. But it also caters to our laziness, and there are businesses out there trying to make it even easier to never get off your ass.

While doing research for this book, I came across an article on "cart abandonment." I thought it was going to be about the lazy asses who don't return their shopping carts to the cart return in the parking lot, which is one of my pet peeves. Instead, it was about a study on why so many people abandon their online shopping carts before completing an online purchase.

The study was conducted by a company called Fast, which the article said provides a "headless" checkout experience. Given my misinterpretation of "cart abandonment" I didn't jump to conclusions. Turns out "headless commerce" is a thing in the retail industry, as is "headless checkout" and "cart abandonment."

In Fast's survey, which polled more than 1,000 adults 18 and older, 86 percent of respondents admitted to abandoning online shopping carts. Reasons included the checkout process being too time-consuming, not wanting to create another online account (the reason I abandoned an online cart recently), not remembering site log-in information, and difficulty inputting their credit card. More than half of the shoppers surveyed said they would be more likely to complete an online purchase if the buying process were simpler.

Fast's technology is designed to make online shopping easier for customers by enabling them to log in without a password and sign in only once on a device. It claims to remember account and payment information without compromising security. Its systems are supposed to improve sales for clients by, among other things, reducing cart abandonment.

"Even in an e-commerce boom, many retailers are still struggling to deliver amazing checkout experiences," says Fast Vice President of Partnerships Calanthia Mei. "Sellers devote a lot of resources to reach shoppers on social media or through digital advertising, only to lose them because of cumbersome checkout options."

Another of my pet peeves, in addition to people who don't return their shopping carts (the real ones) in parking lots, is companies that use the term "amazing" to describe a customer's buying experience. I don't need or expect the experience to be "amazing." I just want to buy this shit. If this is amazing, what am I supposed to call something that is truly amazing? Astounding?

Anyway, it wouldn't have kept me from abandoning my cart on Sephora.com. To buy my wife's perfume online and pick it up later at the store, I had to open a Sephora account and create another God damn password. I decided to just buy it at the store.

Fast co-founder and chief executive officer Domm Holland says his company's technology "unlocks actual functionality. If you see someone wearing a bracelet on television and want to buy it, you can embed a Fast Checkout button to buy it without ever having to leave the screen. The biggest brands are all scrambling for this because before this, there was always a link back to a website, never a connection between native content and commerce."

Not being much of a tech guy, this is a bit over my head. But I think it means that if, for example, you see a recipe for chocolate cake, you can order the cake plate from the same page! Or something like that.

Now that's amazing.

—————— **CHAPTER** ——————

7

Science Fiction and Big Brother

For old folks like me, robots are the stuff of science fiction. But as retail workers at the state and federal level push for a higher minimum wage, robots and other advanced technologies become the retailer's answer. The global robotics market is estimated to reach close to $90 billion by 2025 – *with more than half of that expected to be in the retail market.*

Robots have been used in distribution centers for years, mostly for inventory management. They can check stock levels, identify pricing errors, and locate misplaced items. Amazon reportedly employs more than 100,000 robots in its warehouses to move stock around and help manage supplies. The company says the robots have reduced operating costs 20 percent.

In early 2021, Walmart announced plans to build automated "mini-warehouses" in or adjacent to dozens of its stores. These 20,000 to 30,000 square-foot fulfillment centers will employ robots rather than people to gather certain products ordered by customers and deliver them to an area where actual employees assemble them for customer pickup or delivery. Other products, like produce, meat, and dairy items, are still picked by employees.

Walmart also uses artificial intelligence to help employees select substitute items when an item is not available, and "augmented reality" to map inventory in the storeroom to help employees find things faster. "The idea is to simplify and remove mundane tasks for our associates so they can focus on higher value activities like helping customers," said a Walmart spokesperson.

To deliver products to customers faster, large retailers are experimenting with drones for product delivery. Amazon's Prime Air service promises to deliver items within 30 minutes, provided the product weighs less than five pounds. In 2021, several Kroger supermarkets began piloting (no pun intended) a drone grocery delivery service, teaming up with a company called Drone Express.

Amazon also is accelerating its Key for Business program, in which the company installs a device in apartment buildings that allows its drivers to enter the building without having to buzz. It basically gives Amazon delivery people an electronic key to the building. The company has already installed the device in thousands of apartment buildings across the country. Amazon sells the service to landlords by claiming it cuts down on stolen packages that otherwise would be left outside and reduces noise from the constant buzzing by Amazon delivery people.

McDonald's is piloting artificial intelligence to automate customers' drive-thru orders. A woman's voice will ask if a customer ordering coffee wants cream or sugar, for example, and other follow-up questions. Orders are displayed on a digital screen so customers can ensure they are accurate.

Personally, I don't see who benefits from this other than McDonald's, which may not have to pay as many order-takers. I don't see how customers benefit, especially since the system allegedly gets orders right only about 85 percent of the time. McDonald's CEO Chris Kempczinski says this does not appear to be affecting customer satisfaction ratings.

Really? Fifteen out of every hundred McDonald's customers gets an incorrect order and they don't care? I'd like to see the data on that.

White Castle also is experimenting with automated drive-thru ordering. The burger chain already uses a kitchen robot named Flippy to make fries, chicken rings and mozzarella sticks at some of its locations.

Walmart is eliminating janitors at some of its stores in favor of floor-scrubbing robots that look like a cross between a miniature Zamboni and a motorized wheelchair. The robots can clean floors on their own once they are programmed by a human on the store layout.

Coming soon to a retailer near you are robot store assistants with built-in scanners that can recognize products and call up all kinds of information helpful to customers. They can even lead customers to the product. If the customer needs further assistance, the robot can summon a live employee.

There is something called the "Internet of Things." This too is a thing, with its own acronym (IoT). It basically refers to the interconnectivity and shared-data capabilities of the billions of electronic devices we use to communicate. IoT technology offers retailers the potential to provide what they would call a more engaging and customized shopping experience. For example, at Macy's, when a customer opens the Macy's app on their phone in the store, the app can pinpoint the customer's exact location and direct them to specific offers in the store that they might be interested in based on their buying history.

Macy's also is among retailers using facial recognition technology, again to try to deliver a more personalized shopping experience for its customers. The technology, provided by a company called Clearview, is often used by law enforcement to identify potential crime suspects. It compares crime scene photos with images from Facebook and other social media, where personal information on the individual – including name, address and other details – can be found.

For Macy's, identifying customers gives the company more insight into the types of products the person might be interested in, how much they're likely to spend and other information. The technology also is used to identify shoplifters.

There is artificial intelligence-based software to help online shoppers find that perfect gift based on psychological profiling of the recipient. You answer questions and it gives you suggestions.

Then there is "voice commerce." This too is a thing, with voice commerce sales expected to reach $40 billion in the United States by 2022. Voice assistant technology like Apple's Siri has become commonplace. One survey said as many as 60 million Americans have one of those speakers at which you can bark commands without even having to say please.

Now you can use this technology to order products from Walmart and have them immediately delivered to your door. Walmart's Voice Ordering service enables customers sitting on their asses eating out of Styrofoam containers in front of the TV to say, "Hey Siri, add a bag of Cheetos, a box of Ex-lax and a tube of Chapstick to my Walmart cart." A half-hour later, the products arrive.

Some people find use of facial recognition, voice prints, and customer identification technology a bit nefarious. For example, a woman in Illinois who describes herself as "a regular customer of Macy's" filed a class action lawsuit against the company charging invasion of privacy based on their use of facial recognition technology. The lawsuit alleges that Macy's has run thousands of customer images from its security footage through Clearview's database and that "any Macy's employee with access to the surveillance database could use it for their own personal ends – for example, to stalk or track an individual."

There also have been studies that show facial recognition services, talking digital assistants and other artificial intelligence-based technologies to be biased against women and people of color. The problem, it seems, is that these automated technologies are developed by humans, primarily white men. Yet the solutions being proposed all seem to center on more regular oversight of these technologies by these same humans, so not sure this will fix the problem.

People have expressed privacy and security concerns over Amazon's Key for Business program as well. Landlords who have installed the device say it is safer than giving out security codes. Amazon says it does background checks on its delivery people and they can only unlock doors if they have a package to scan.

Amazon doesn't charge to install its device, but most of these other advanced technologies are expensive, making cost the main obstacle to broader application. Many of these technologies also are not successful in the long run. Companies invest millions to pilot technologies that they end up not implementing because they find they don't cut costs or improve service enough to warrant the expense.

A 2019 report by business consulting firm McKinsey & Co. estimated that about half the activities in the retail industry can be automated with current technology. But only about 5 percent of jobs can be fully automated. Companies will continue to explore the technical, ethical, and economic issues around artificial intelligence and other technologies and implement what makes business sense.

In the meantime, we should keep in mind how our personal information is being used when we order products on the Internet, sign up for a company loyalty program, and open the apps on our phones. Someone may be watching.

—— CHAPTER ——
8

"The Customer is Always Right!" (No, they're not.)

Someone posted on the Retail Life Facebook page that a woman in England called the police because her ice cream didn't have enough sprinkles. "Sounds like a Karen," someone replied.

Any job in which you must deal with the public takes great restraint. There are just enough assholes out there to make life miserable for the rest of us.

The "Karen" meme is used in the retail world to describe some of these customers. Know Your Meme, an online meme dictionary, defines Karen as "a pejorative slang term for an obnoxious, angry, entitled, and often racist middle-aged woman who uses her privilege to get her way or police other people's behaviors."

In retail, these customers feel entitled because of their self-perceived buying power. They expect the threat "I will never shop here again!" to strike fear in minimum wage hourly employees. News flash: It doesn't.

"I don't understand customers who threaten to take their business elsewhere, like I care," says one employee. "Please do!"

The Karen term has been criticized as racist since it usually refers to white women. But retail employees use it to describe a customer's behavior more than their looks.

"Usually, the meme is associated with lower-stakes situations, like a person at an Applebee's who got the wrong meal," says Matt Schimkowitz, senior editor at Know Your Meme.

The Karen moniker allegedly originated from a cut on a 2005 comedy album by comedian Dane Cook called "The Friend Nobody Likes."

"There is one person in every group of friends that nobody likes," Cook says. In an example, he used the name Karen. "When she's not around, you just look at each other and say, 'God, Karen, she's such a douchebag!'"

"The customer is always right … as long as they know what the fuck they are talking about," says one retail employee. "I work for an auto parts retailer. A customer recently had a meltdown because we didn't have parts for her stove!"

Some of the worst Karen incidents occur when a customer wants to return a product for which they don't have a receipt, that has been used, and in some cases may not have even come from that store.

"I'm working Guest Services and a woman insists on returning a vacuum that did not come from our store. She didn't have a receipt, obviously. The vacuum looked about two years old and had clearly been used. 'So, you're calling me a liar?' she says. She proceeded to call me every name in the book. Then she picked up a stapler and threw it at me. There were some toys on the counter and she shoved those to the ground. She caused quite a scene."

Employees would at least like to have store management's support in dealing with all the Karens. Often, they do not.

"I think what I hate most about retail is they have all these rules, saying what customers are and are not allowed to do, and the company will have your back if things go wrong. But as soon as the customer threatens to never come back to the store, they throw all of that out the window, let the customer have their way, and often punish you!"

"The Number One rule customers should commit to memory: You don't run nothin' up in here," says one employee defiantly. "Not today. Not ever."

Retail employee websites, Facebook pages and other social media are replete with examples of Karen incidents and other crazy customer requests.

"I had a lady ask me to put a couple of outfits she'd picked out on clearance so she could afford to buy them."

"Had a lady ask me if she could borrow a few pairs of shoes from the store so she could walk around in each pair for a day or two to see which she liked best. Then she'd buy the pair she liked and give the others back."

"I had a woman ask for a refund on a jacket that she cut the arms off of. She said now it didn't look right."

"A woman wanted me to just give her Percocet because her dentist wanted her to have it but didn't write her a prescription."

"A man asked me where we sold our ants, as he had bought his son an ant farm. I told him we didn't sell ants but he was welcome to check our break room."

"When working at Claire's, a woman wanted me – a barely qualified retail employee – to pull out the deeply infected and embedded earrings in her eight-year-old daughter's ears because I was the one who pierced them three weeks prior. They had done no after-care or precautionary steps to prevent problems, then told me it was my fault."

"A lady asked me to be her personal shopper. She handed me a list and said she would wait in the fitting room while I picked out some things for her to try on. I told her I would love to be able to do that but I had a department to look after and other customers who needed my help. She wasn't offended but surprised that I couldn't just drop everything for her."

"At my old job we had rotisserie chicken. A lady asked me if I could just give her a cooked chicken that wasn't rotisserie. I told her this was the only way we cooked them. She said she knew that 'but when you package it can you just have it say cooked chicken, not rotisserie, because otherwise my kids won't eat it.' I told her I can't change preprinted packages so she said she would just buy it elsewhere. Ten minutes later she was back to get the chicken."

"Had a regular Lotto mutant want me to help him move."

"Former zoo employee here. A guest asked if they could pet the baby hippo."

"At my old job, the bathroom was out of order so some old guy asked if he could just pee on the wall in the stockroom."

"A refrigerator was on back order. This woman who wanted it already had one but wanted a new one. The manufacturer said three months minimum. She told me I should go to a competitor and buy her the fridge myself because it's $800 more expensive at those places and she shouldn't have to pay more."

"We had a badly damaged chair reduced to $100, floor model only. This woman wanted me to get her a new one or like new and sell it to her for $100 because the floor model had too much damage but she doesn't want to pay $1590 for a new one."

"This lady brought her dog in and it pooped on a carpet that we sell. I told her she would have to buy it. She refused and called the police, saying we were harassing her. The police came, gave her a citation, and she was banned from the store. The rug cost $1,000. The company sent her a bill."

"Today I had a guy come through my line with a pack of beef sticks that cost $17.99. When I scanned them, they came up $15.99. He wanted me to add $2 so it matched the price on the shelf. I said to myself, you've got to be kidding me. I called my supervisor over. After confirming that this guy did indeed want to pay $2 more than he had to, she gave him the sticks for free."

"I got yelled at by a customer because his food was late getting to him. Basically, the order was done and his number was called but he didn't respond. After several more tries, the order got thrown in the waste. Then he comes up asking where his order is and shows me his receipt. My manager had his order remade. In the meantime, the customer is railing at me that this was somehow my fault. I told him he could have listened for his number and come up 30 minutes earlier. I don't think he's coming back."

"Man, reading through this feed I'm so happy I work behind the counter in a gun shop. Only thing anyone ever bitches to me about here is the price of ammo."

Having an arsenal of guns behind you might also have something to do with it.

—— CHAPTER ——
9

Stopping the Steal

When I was in fourth grade, I was in a department store with a friend shopping for a Father's Day gift for my dad. There was a bottle of Brut cologne for $5 and a bottle of Old Spice for $3.50. I removed the $5 price tag from the Brut and replaced it with the $3.50 price tag from the Old Spice. I had seen my dad do this – switch price tags on products – many times. There were no bar codes or scanners in those days. The cashier simply rang up the price on the sticker.

As soon as the transaction was complete – as my friend and I laughed over getting a $5 bottle of cologne for $3.50 – a burly store detective grabbed my arm and took us into a back room where they called our moms to pick us up. At first, I denied everything, claiming the wrong price tag was already on the Brut and I was the victim of a horrible miscarriage of justice. But the store detective had seen everything and at some point on the ride home I finally owned up to it to my mom.

"Wait till your father gets home!" she threatened. And that was scary. My dad had a booming voice and a rough background. Let's just say he had done worse things in his life than change price tags.

So, I am up in my bedroom when I hear my dad come home. I hear him coming up the stairs. He walks into my room.

"Your mother told me what you did," he said in his booming voice. "I've got just one thing to say." Pause. "I'm glad you got me the Brut."

That was it! I learned later from my sisters that my mom was much angrier at my dad than she was at me. She blamed him for the whole thing because she knew I had seen him switch price tags. But I didn't blame my dad. When I saw him switch price tags, I knew it was wrong, and I knew it was wrong for me to do it. Maybe it did make it seem more acceptable to me subconsciously, though.

I had shoplifted other things like candy and baseball cards before this incident but never again. At first it was because I was afraid to get caught again. But eventually it was because I decided that stealing is just plain wrong. I don't believe in a lot of rules in life but there were two I gave my kids: you don't hurt people, and you don't take shit that doesn't belong to you.

My kids, like me, didn't abide by this. My daughter got caught shoplifting when she was in junior high school. My son just never got caught. It is almost as if shoplifting is as benign a transgression in our society as going a few miles over the speed limit. Except shoplifting is *stealing*. It is not a victimless crime. It hurts business and makes everyone pay higher prices. It can reduce employment levels and cost employee jobs. How do you justify it? How do you live with yourself?

What makes shoplifters think they should be entitled to just walk into a place and take shit without paying for it? I know, I did it. But I was in fourth grade. My kids were adolescents. There are adults who do this for a living! And we're supposed to be okay with that? I'm not.

Most shoplifters do justify it. They believe they're entitled to take shit without paying for it because the big evil corporations that own the stores are ripping us off and they can afford it. If the shoplifter is a minority, they may feel entitled because they've been victims of discrimination. Then there are people who simply have no morals. Few shoplifters do it out of financial necessity, although approximately 3 percent of shoplifters are professionals who steal for resale or profit, according to the National Shoplifting Prevention Coalition.

Shoplifting is the biggest cause of retail "shrinkage." The average shrink percentage in the retail industry is about 2 percent of sales. Other causes of shrinkage include employee theft, paperwork errors, and supplier fraud.

According to the National Association for Shoplifting Prevention, more than 500,000 shoplifting incidents occur in the United States *each day*. This results in more than $35 million in losses *each day*. The Lufthansa heist – the largest armed robbery in U.S. history – netted about $5 million. This is like seven Lufthansa heists *each day*. Annually, shoplifting costs retailers more than $13 *billion*.

Concealing and walking off with merchandise is the most common form of shoplifting, although some shoplifters don't even bother concealing.

"Some people just walk out of the store with their cart," says one store manager. "They just boldly fill it up and walk out."

Nowadays, when everyone has a cell phone, it is easy for criminals inside the store to communicate with each other and with cohorts outside the store to make fast getaways and execute other coordinated schemes.

When stores started putting sensors on certain products, thieves would use aluminum foil-lined bags to shield the product from setting off the detector. That no longer works. Now when someone steals something with a sensor, the alarm will go off. But a thief won't care.

"They know we can't come out of the store after them," says one retail employee. "So unless there is an armed guard at the door, they will get away and just cut the sensor off later on their own. There also are many instances where the sensor goes off and the customer is completely innocent. Maybe they didn't notice it on the product or didn't know someone from the store had to take it off."

Of course, the honest person will usually stop and hesitate and might even re-enter the store and show their receipt. The ones that pick up their pace probably stole something, although some honest people also might just keep going because they know they didn't steal anything or do anything wrong.

Beauty items are high-theft items because they are small and pocketable. At the Walmart near me, the beauty section has its own turnstile that you must go through, and you have to pay for items there rather than at the main registers. This Walmart has a lot of stuff locked up. Men's work shirts. Baby formula. Even men's underwear. You have to summon a store employee to get those items. At the Target near me, they lock up more of the higher-end items, like baby monitors, vacuums, computers and small electronics.

Some professional shoplifters make a lucrative living. One famous case involved a middle-aged couple and their adult daughter. They lived in a million-dollar home in a posh north shore suburb of Chicago. They were caught with $74,000 worth of stolen dolls, toys, cosmetics, and other items in their car coming off a shoplifting spree through Maryland, Louisiana, Texas, Oklahoma, Tennessee, and Florida.

These people allegedly had been doing this for at least a decade, stealing as much as $10 million in merchandise and netting at least $4 million on the sale of that merchandise through eBay and other channels. They ultimately pled guilty to conspiracy and fraud charges, including interstate transportation of stolen property, and all served time in prison. While the family disputed the amount of merchandise they were accused of stealing, there was plenty of surveillance video showing the mother stashing items into pockets inside a long skirt. In one Houston mall, the family was seen making off with about $12,000 worth of merchandise without being stopped by security.

Most professionals who make their living doing this tend to not spend a lot of time in the store. They tend to get in and out quickly. In a recent incident in that same posh north shore suburb of Chicago, about 10 people stormed a Neiman Marcus store and stole purses displayed near the entryway. Witnesses said it took less than a minute for the thieves to run off with all the purses.

"That's not unusual," says one store manager. "There are groups that will storm a store like Gap, for example, and grab all the jeans off the front table. The idea is that there are so many of them that even if the store had a security guard, they couldn't catch all of them. When I worked at a sporting goods store, we had North Face jackets on a rack that were triple-sensored and actually locked to the rack. We had one group come in, create a distraction, and then just wheel the whole rack out, alarms be damned. They are gone in an instant."

"Sometimes these groups come from out of state," says a retail employee who works at a mall near the airport. "There would be people who would grab stuff right before they were to get on a plane. Just put it right in their suitcase and take off."

Some stores "trespass" known shoplifters. Once they're trespassed, they're not allowed to be on the premises. If they come into the store, they can be arrested for trespassing. But even then, the person has to be in the store long enough for the police to come, which is usually not the case.

Experienced store personnel can spot most shoplifters immediately. The problem is that most employees would rather look the other way while the rest aren't allowed to do anything. Store policies benefit the shoplifter and shoplifters know this. At most stores, employees can't confront a shoplifter. They have to call Security or Loss Prevention, and by the time they get there, the shoplifter is gone.

With all the loss they suffer, you would think retailers would take shoplifting more seriously instead of simply chalking it up as a cost of doing business. Instead, there is a trend away from shoplifter apprehension and prosecution due to the time, cost, and legal liability issues involved. Examples of what employees face:

"I saw an African American woman put shoes in her bag and begin to walk out of the store. I asked her to return them or I'd call Security. The woman just ignored me and left with the shoes. Then she called the company and complained she was profiled because of her race. So the company fired me! The official reason was because I had left the store to confront the shoplifter. But the fact this person blatantly stole merchandise from the store meant nothing to the company."

"There was this group of teens who would steal from the store and come back to shop the same day or that week and wear the clothes they just stole. We couldn't confront them or stop them from leaving. It was very frustrating."

"It was closing time. A guy who seemed to be on something grabbed a bunch of clothes and went into a fitting room. He left the store with one of our shirts draped over his shoulder and a pair of shoes. I yelled at him to give the stuff back. First, he said it wasn't ours. Then he threw it at me. I was written up for that. Part of it is for our safety. But I still wish we could confront people."

"Has anyone else ever had someone shove their camera in your face? I was watching these two girls who seemed suspicious, from very far away while doing my job. Next thing I know, one of the girls sticks her phone cam in my face and asks, 'What's your name?' She notes my name badge and says I'm accusing her of stealing, which just makes her look more guilty. So I walk to the front to make sure their bags get checked. The girl walks up to me, calls me names and threatens to punch me. I stood there letting her dig herself deeper while noting that we have cameras capturing the whole thing."

Sometimes, the shoplifters get violent.

"One afternoon, my manager confronted a shoplifter in the back of the store and asked her to leave. She left in a fit of rage, destroying every display she could get her hands on as she ran out of the store, tossing armfuls of hangers on the floor and ruining carefully folded table displays as we all looked on in horror."

"I worked at a Dollar Store and saw a lady put a glass bottle of perfume down her pants. When I told her to take the bottle out of her pants and pay for it, she pulled it out and threw it at me."

In July 2021, retailers in several cities across California began closing their stores early due a rise in shoplifting. Target stores in San Francisco, for example, started closing at 6 p.m. instead of 10 p.m. This clearly would cost the company sales, but apparently the level of theft was worse.

"For more than a month, we've been experiencing a significant and alarming rise in theft and security incidents at our San Francisco stores, similar to reports from other retailers in the area," said Target spokesman Brian Harper-Tibaldo.

Walgreens closed 17 locations in San Francisco due to what it calls rampant theft. The company said the level of theft in these stores was more than four times the national average. It spent 35 times more on security and still had to close the stores. CVS reported similar problems.

"We lost the flagship Gap in Union Square," said San Francisco Supervisor Ahsha Safai of another store that closed due to excessive stealing. "If we don't deal with organized retail crime, I fear many other stores will close."

While a national more than a local problem, the increase in shoplifting in California is due at least in part to a controversial law passed a few years ago that made shoplifting less then $950 worth of merchandise a misdemeanor instead of a felony. The retail chain Safeway blames the law for "dramatic increases" in retail theft. An editorial in the *Las Vegas Review-Journal* lambasted California lawmakers for promoting a law that emboldens shoplifters and warned Nevada policymakers to not make the same mistake.

"There's nothing wrong with trying to clear the jails of nonviolent offenders. But advertising that certain types of criminal acts won't be pursued or prosecuted shows a disregard for law-abiding citizens and is an open invitation to habitual criminals and a recipe for neighborhood decline."

If it was me, I'd hire more full-time security, maybe off-duty cops, and take other strong-arm measures to intimidate and stop would-be shoplifters. But in addition to the expense, I guess there are other problems with that.

"Our priority is the safety of our employees and consumers," says Rachel Michelin, president and chief executive officer of the California Retailer's Association. "We can't have our security guards going after this. They are not law enforcement."

In many stores I researched, security guards are not allowed to engage with shoplifters.

"Obviously they don't want ourselves or anybody else to get injured while we're out here attempting to make these apprehensions and to leave it to law enforcement," said one security guard at a San Francisco-based Walgreens who has no problem with this policy given that it is not unusual for professional criminals to carry weapons. "I don't have any intention of getting stabbed for $60 worth of stuff."

A lesser problem, but still a problem, is employee theft. It was gratifying to find out that in most stores, stealing by employees is not tolerated.

"We spend more time trying to manage internal theft than we do on shoplifting," said one store manager. "I'm surprised there is so much because in our store there are cameras everywhere."

And it's not always the hourly employees.

"One day our district manager came to our store out of the blue. This was unusual because she always gave us notice. Turns out the cameras caught our general manager stealing $400 out of the petty cash drawer. Apparently, she had been doing this for a while. They fired her that day before we opened."

Despite the presence of cameras, the majority of employee theft happens at – where else? – self-checkout.

"They'll take five things up there, scan one, put all five in a bag, pay and walk out," one manager says. "The thing is, you can pull up the transaction. The cameras can see what you paid for and what you walked away with. As an employee of the store, you should know this. But they do it anyway."

One store manager who works in a mall says a few years ago, employees of his store and other stores in the mall conspired to allow each other to steal from each other's stores.

"A guy who works at Polo, for example, would come into your store with an empty shopping bag and your employee would look the other way while the Polo guy filled his bag with merchandise and walked out. Then your employee would go to Polo and take something while the Polo guy looked the other way. The food court people might give you free pizza. Everyone, it seemed, was in on it."

The crime ring was ultimately discovered by mall management and the individual stores involved.

"My district manager tells me we're going to fire everyone and start fresh," the store manager says. "So I go in early. I have to ring Security to get in. I tell Security where I work. He says, 'Oh, that's where you can get a free whatever.' That's how widespread this was. Who knows, maybe even Security was involved."

When it came time to hire new staff, this manager says there was one automatic deal-breaker.

"If anyone applying for a job listed any other store in the mall in their past experience, I didn't hire them."

For most store employees and law-abiding shoppers, the amount of retail theft that goes on is demoralizing. While sensors, surveillance cameras, and other measures have helped reduce losses, shoplifting is a tough problem to crack. If taking shit without paying for it is really what you want to do, it's not hard and you'll probably get away with it. Shoplifters are caught only about once every 50 times and more than half of those caught are not prosecuted.

What I'm left with after all this is, one, how do these people live with themselves, but also, it's not like this stuff takes no effort. You can make a living any number of ways, but at least with a regular job you don't have to worry about your conscience. That is, if you have one. If not, shoplifting is for you.

——— CHAPTER ———
10

Many Happy Returns

Speaking of effort, returning stolen goods for a refund takes a good deal, along with a lot of chutzpah. But this is a common practice among shoplifters.

"People grab receipts off the ground or from the garbage outside the store, then they come in, steal the product, and try to return it for a refund using the receipt," says one store manager.

This works fine for the thief if the person who bought the product used cash. Even if they used a debit card, some stores give you cash back for that as well. (I don't know why they would do this instead of requiring that the refund go back to the card, but some stores do offer this option).

If the purchaser used a credit card, however, most stores apply the credit directly back to that card, which doesn't do the thief any good.

"Unless they ask for a gift card instead," says the manager.

Whoa! What? They can do that? Why on Earth are they allowed to do that?

"Most stores will ask to see the credit card before they will apply the refund to a gift card," she says. "If you don't have the credit card, many stores will offer a merchandise credit. Even if you're trying to return stolen merchandise without a receipt, they may still give you a merchandise credit. The thieves then sell these 'merch credits' for cash."

These stores are too nice. Why they would give someone who has no receipt or any proof whatsoever that they purchased the product a merchandise credit is beyond me.

"Most stores limit the number of items you can return, with or with-out a receipt," the manager says. "In most stores, if you don't have a receipt, you at least need an ID to return something. Then when your license is scanned, it's put into a system, and if your returns exceed whatever the company's dollar limit is, there will be a prompt at the register that you have exceeded your return limit."

Then, of course, the crook will try to get someone else to return the stolen goods, paying some random guy a few bucks to go in and use his ID to get a merchandise credit.

"At one store where I worked, if you were returning something without a receipt, you were given a merch credit for the lowest price on the item over the past 90 days, not the face value of the product," says one store manager. "One time a person who was clearly paid to come in and do a no-receipt return – some kid to whom they said, 'Could you do me a favor? I lost my ID. Could you just take this in and get a merchandise credit?' – came in with an expensive item. We looked it up and could only give him something like a $10 merch card for a $100 item. So then the person who couldn't return the item came in with the merch credit and wanted to buy back the item with the merch credit! We said no, can't do that."

Of course, these people shouldn't get anything because they stole the stuff in the first place. Yet they are always indignant when they are denied.

"A lot of stores have beefed up their return policies, but sometimes if the person gets angry enough or shouts loud enough, it gets overridden," one manager says.

And it's not just shoplifters who try to do no-receipt returns or get something for nothing.

"When I worked at Ulta, someone tried to return some liter-sized bottles of shampoo and conditioner that had clearly been refilled with water, so we refused them. They proceeded to call Corporate and complain. They got a $100 gift certificate. We got bitched at."

"At Little Caesars, this lady came in with her pizza box and told the cashier she had bought the pizza the previous day and it was burnt so she wanted a new one. There were only two slices left in the box and it was two days old yet they still gave her a new pizza."

"At Aldi, they had a return policy where you get your money back plus an item of equal or lesser value. One customer routinely returned a gallon of milk with just a quarter remaining, claiming it was 'rancid.' He'd then get a new gallon and his money back. This went on for weeks until the district manager put his foot down."

"A woman came in, grabbed an herb-roasted rotisserie chicken, plopped down in the casual seating area, ate 85 percent of it with her bare hands, then brought the carcass to Customer Service and tried to return it."

"When I worked at a gas station, a guy came in, grabbed a foot-long sub from the sandwich case, opened it up, pulled a hair out of his own head, stuffed it in the sandwich, then came up to the register and demanded a refund."

"A customer brought back a jumpsuit for a refund because it had shit on it. She claimed it was like that when she bought it. It really stunk and there was no way it would have gone unnoticed at the time of sale. Yet someone at the refund counter actually accepted it and put it back in the trolley full of other returned items for us to put back out. There was a note stapled to it that said, 'Warning: feces inside.'"

"At Nordstrom, they allowed cash back for any return. A lady came in with a pile of clothes from the '90s. We still gave her cash back. Then she pulled out a coat with a tag so old our register couldn't read it. It turned out to be her dead grandmother's coat and she wanted cash for it."

"A customer came in to return some lightbulbs he said were defective. I was new and wasn't sure of the return policy on certain items without a receipt so I asked my boss and he said no. The customer got so angry he ended up throwing the lightbulbs – which weren't in their package – directly at our heads. After my boss chased him out of the store, he called later and threatened to kill us!"

"I once saw someone trying to return an empty 10-pound bag of ice because it had melted too quickly."

"I had a woman try to return something without even bringing in the item!"

Gift card scams have received some publicity in recent years. These are scams against gullible people, not retailers. It doesn't matter to retailers who buys and uses their gift cards. Yet because of these scams, most stores now limit the amount you can purchase in gift cards. Here's how it typically works:

It is often elderly people who are targeted as they are thought to be and probably are more vulnerable. They'll be told their grandson is in trouble and needs money to get out of jail or for a ride back home. Or it's the IRS and if you don't pay this right now, you are going to lose your house. Or it's the local sheriff saying you didn't pay a past-due ticket and unless you do, they are going to arrest you.

At this point you might ask where gift cards come in. Well, to settle these financial obligations, the scammers tell the person to go to a store – any store that sells gift cards – and buy a gift card. They will often stay on the phone with the person while they do this. Then the person is supposed to read the numbers off the gift card to the scammer so the scammer can use the gift card to settle the debt.

I am told these people are very convincing. But I am a senior and I can't think of a scenario where a stranger calls me out of the blue, describes some situation I must immediately pay my way out of, tells me to go out and buy a gift card and read them the numbers off it, and I do it. No matter how convincing they are, no matter what the story is, I cannot think of a set of circumstances that would prompt me to do this. Of course, I wouldn't even answer the phone. I never do if I don't recognize the number. But victims of this must be incredibly stupid.

The scammers use the information from the gift cards to order merchandise online. When the people who are scammed realize they were scammed, they often come back to the store where they bought the gift card, say they were scammed, and want their money back. Uh, sorry. The store didn't scam you out of anything. If you want retribution, you'll have to get it from the scammer, which at that point is impossible. Next time don't be so stupid.

In addition to now limiting how much in gift cards you can buy, stores also now post warnings of these scams online. Cashiers are briefed. All to protect idiots from their own stupidity because none of this harms the store. It's to protect *you*, dumb ass! Whether you buy the gift card and the scammer redeems it or I buy the gift card and my daughter redeems it, it's the same to the retailer.

Speaking of stupid, there have even been store clerks that have been victimized by the following scam, although this employee was not:

"I was working Customer Service. Part of my job was to answer incoming phone calls. We got a call from a guy claiming he was from Technical Support. He said he wanted to update our systems and to do so I needed to follow his instructions. I knew this was a scam but decided to play along. He told me to log into our computer, ring up a gift card for $100, say he paid cash, then read off the gift card number for him. He said that would update our systems! Still the funniest scam attempt I've ever seen."

As long as you don't fall for it.

— CHAPTER —

11

"Kids will be kids!"

"To the woman with five screaming kids wondering how the box of condoms got in her cart: You're welcome!"

When I was a kid, my mom often dragged me with her when she went shopping at department stores or women's clothing stores. I would be bored stiff and must have acted out because I remember my mom threatening on more than one occasion to give me a bare-ass spanking right in the middle of the store!

When I got older, my friends and I would go to the Old Orchard Shopping Center and wreak havoc on a Saturday. One time, we found these laugh boxes in the Marshall Field's toy department and went around the store setting them off behind unsuspecting customers and watching their reactions.

We didn't vandalize or anything like that, but we were obnoxious and treated these retail establishments like a playground before often being told to leave. We would spend a whole Saturday amusing ourselves annoying retail salespeople and customers with no intention of ever buying anything. Whatever money we had we usually spent on food. The cafeteria on top of the Montgomery Ward store was a favorite because you could get a cheeseburger, fries and Coke for a dollar.

Teenagers today still wreak havoc on retail establishments. Some take the whole "store as playground" concept to an even higher level.

"I used to work at a large sporting goods store," says one store manager. "We had full-size basketball hoops, bats and balls, treadmills. High school kids would come in and I had to chase them out all the time because they were playing basketball in the store, goofing around on the treadmill, with absolutely no intention of buying anything."

Kids playing hide and seek in the store seems to be common, often among teens. Or scavenger hunts in the mall.

"The mall I worked at actually had to implement a policy prohibiting these birthday party scavenger hunts that had become popular," says one mall employee. "The kids were given a list of things to find in the mall and they would go to the various stores to look for them. When they'd find an item, they'd take a picture. That was the general concept, anyway.

"So you'd have 12 sixth-grade girls trying on high heels and taking pictures of each other for their birthday party scavenger hunt, with no intent to buy. This was so disruptive. And these things were often on Saturday when the mall was extra busy. So the mall had to outlaw scavenger hunts in the mall."

Everyone who has worked retail, it seems, has had to endure younger children causing chaos, with their parents often complicit.

"When there is a toy department, they just let the kids take the toys off the shelves, bounce the balls, ride whatever, with no intent to purchase," says one store manager. "It's just to keep their kids occupied, like we're an on-site daycare center. And then they just leave all the stuff all over the floor and we have to clean up after them."

Some parents will give their child a toy to play with while they are in the store, then when they get up to the register, they tell the cashier on the sly, "no, we don't want that" after their kid has chewed on it. This seems to happen a lot.

"When I worked at Walmart a lady came in with her toddler who absolutely destroyed the clothing racks, throwing a ton of stuff on the floor. I heard her tell him, 'Go ahead, Sweetie, these people get paid to clean up after you.'"

"In the late '90s I was managing a video store and a woman was letting her kids trash the place. It came to a head when one kid, around 4 years old, took a shit on the floor! His mother stood there laughing about how 'cute' he was."

"I saw a trail of cereal going through the store. As I swept it up, I eventually came upon the source — a 4-year-old child with a baggie, just tossing the cereal on the ground as he walked. When the mom saw me with the sweeper, she smiled and said, 'Kids will be kids!'"

"One day at Bath & Body Works, a mom walked in with her child. He ran all over the store and messed around with all the products. Pretty standard 'mom isn't paying attention' behavior, not too crazy. But then when I was ringing her up, this kid flings his entire body across the counter to behind the register where I was standing. He then proceeds to start licking my elbow! I knew I couldn't touch him or push him off in any way, so I just looked at the mom hoping she would do something. She just laughed and said, 'Oh, he does that sometimes.'"

"Has any cashier told a kid to get their hand off the belt and their parent told you to not discipline their kid because it's their job?" asks a grocery store cashier. "I was told that today. That kid might've gotten his hand stuck on the belt. I might've saved the kid's life. The customer should be thankful."

Then there are kids whose parents lose track of them, and of course the parents blame the store. Even in a small store like Hallmark, relates one store manager.

"One particular day, the mall was busy. It was Christmas season. This kid, about three years old, just walked out of the store. We didn't see him. He was left unattended and the mom had absolutely no clue. All the sudden she is in a panic running around looking for her kid. I think one of the other customers said they thought he may have walked out of the store and the mom goes into a raging screaming fit as if it was our fault. So we called mall security."

Turns out the kid took the escalator down to the first floor where Santa Claus and the mall's Christmas display was located. The woman angrily blamed the store for not watching her kid rather than herself for not watching her kid.

The best "kid gets lost" story I heard was from a stand-alone Famous Footwear not located in a mall. A woman came in with a small boy and was trying on shoes. While she was doing this, the boy was bopping around the store, climbing on the benches, ducking behind the rows of shoes, playing a hide-and-seek kind of thing.

"The mom is laughing, although I'm not paying much attention because I'm helping customers," says an employee on duty that day. "As I'm at the register ringing someone out, the woman panics. 'Have you seen my son?' I said no but that he could not have gone out the front door because I was right there."

They start looking for the boy down every aisle. In the meantime, the woman is getting more and more panicked. She calls 911. She pushes open the emergency door in back, which sets off that alarm. She is literally screaming her son's name.

The kid was in the store the whole time. He had crawled into the bottom shelf in one of the aisles.

"I think the more panicked the mom got, the more scared he was to come out," the employee says. "He was literally all the way in the back. You pretty much had to be on the floor to see him. The woman was hugging him for dear life when the police showed up."

Then there are the kids' birthday parties.

"I worked at a children's store that hosted birthday parties. During a disastrous party that was already spiraling out of control, one of the kids kicked over the table with their cake on it after being told it wasn't yet time for cake. The mom, who was a monster herself, blamed me. She then dragged me around the store by my arm to 'apologize to her babies' and then punched me. The company gave the family free gifts, a new free cake, and a completely free party. I put in my two weeks' notice."

——— **C H A P T E R** ———

12

No Call/No Show

In most businesses other than retail, employee attendance is not an issue. Having worked in corporate office environments most of my professional life, I can attest that few employees ever missed work for anything other than scheduled vacations and the occasional sick day. Even when you were sick or had a sick child, you would usually say you'd be "working from home." Someone simply not showing up or coming up with the excuses retail employees so often use to justify why they suddenly can't work on a day they're scheduled was unheard of.

Most retail employees don't have the option of working from home, so perhaps this comparison is unfair. Still, I find the number of call offs and no shows in retail alarming. In the Walmart and Target stores I researched, the number of employees missing work on any given day averages about 10 percent. In other words, if 100 employees are scheduled, only about 90 show up for work.

"Some don't even call," says one store manager. "They just don't show up."

Even on new-employee orientation day, only three of six employees at one store showed up and received their orientation. "One of the others just never showed up at all," says the store manager. "The other two came but didn't have the proper materials we had asked them to bring."

How many times does an employee have to blatantly play hooky from work before they're fired? At large retailers, you're often allowed up to three attendance issues in your first 90 days before they let you go.

"First, we have to talk to them and ask them if they knew they were scheduled for the day they didn't show up," says one store manager. "Then we tell them that if they continue to have issues, there may be corrective action. After three no call, no shows, it's considered job abandonment."

The impact when people call off is that the rest of the employees, "or in most cases the store manager, has to work 12-hour days to make up for it," says one store manager. So why give employees so much rope?

Companies are afraid of lawsuits, which they shouldn't be, given that most employers have the right to terminate any employee for no cause, let alone a legitimate cause like attendance. As long as there is no discrimination, the employer is in the clear. But no one wants to be sued so retailers tend to give employees a ridiculous number of chances.

Speaking of ridiculous, if retail employees think their employers buy their lame excuses for missing work, they are wrong.

The most common excuse for missing work is the so-called "family emergency." Retail employees seem to have an inordinate number of family emergencies. Some employees have multiple family emergencies a year. It is rarely specific, like my mother had a heart attack and was rushed to the hospital or my son fell down the stairs and is in traction. Just a family emergency. Of course, most family emergencies in retail are bullshit and your manager knows it.

"A lot of car trouble," says one store manager, citing another common excuse. "Flat tire. Car won't start."

"Pet emergencies are big," says another.

"Food poisoning. That's probably second only to family emergencies at our store."

"I had an employee call and say he couldn't come in because the power was out and he couldn't get out of his garage. So I said, 'See that big red handle hanging from your garage door opener to emergency release your garage door?' He didn't work for me much longer after that."

"We had a person call off because they said they needed a mental health day."

"Or how about the employee who makes up some excuse as to why they can't come in and then their mom calls looking for them, blowing their cover?"

Many employees use the excuse that they were out of town and couldn't get back in time.

"Then you see pictures of them on Facebook at a local bar or some community event and wonder, are they really that stupid?" says one manager. "Some employees are savvy enough to limit who can see their posts on Facebook, Snapchat, Instagram and so on. Some are not and so are shocked when you find proof that they're lying."

Yet most of these employees don't lose their jobs. In the Facebook era, employees are constantly spotted in posts from bars, beaches, parties and other venues when they were supposed to be out of town or dealing with some emergency. First offenses are usually tolerated with just a mild reprimand from your boss.

"One employee allegedly had COVID six times!" one manager told me. "And she got paid for all six times."

"We've had people punch in, leave, then come back and punch out, and they were never here," says another.

"A lot of people, after they've worked a few weeks, suddenly decide they need Sundays off to go to church. Or they can't work nights because they're studying for school."

"Swapping shifts is a big thing. We recently had a girl who all week was looking for someone to cover her shift. Then she called out with a medical emergency. When you call off with an emergency on a day that you had wanted to swap a shift, that kind of affects your credibility. She quit the next day."

Maybe there is something about being hourly that makes these employees feel like attendance is optional? Maybe it's the low pay, bad conditions and having to deal with customers all day? Would they take their jobs more seriously if they were on salary or commission?

"When I started in retail, I worked on commission," says one retail veteran who worked in a men's clothing store. "This was maybe 30 years ago. You got a base salary of $65 a week and anything else you got was from commissions on your sales. If you weren't there, you couldn't sell anything. So in those days, we didn't really have an attendance problem."

The size of the store and number of employees is surely a variable. When I worked at Best & Co., I shared the nighttime and weekend shipping clerk/stock boy position with one other person. If one of us couldn't make it, we'd switch days. Neither of us would have dreamed of just not coming in or leaving the store without either of us on a given day if we could help it. I'm sure it's different in a retail store with 200 employees.

The majority of people who work at retailers like Walmart and Target are younger people, mostly part time, many still in high school, and few who consider this job a career or even a significant steppingstone to a career.

"They might be working to save a few bucks for college," says one manager. "But obviously many of them don't need the money that badly given the amount of absenteeism. A lot of them, the younger ones, don't care because the money isn't a necessity or they think they can get another job just like that. And unfortunately, they probably can."

When you cut through the shit, this whole issue is really due to the fact that most of these workers are young part-timers and this isn't going to be their career so they don't care. A lot of them are going to school. A lot of them still live at home with their parents. And if you insist on cheap labor – if this is the employee pool retailers have decided to tap to fill these jobs – this is what you're going to get.

The characteristics of the typical retail job – part time, low pay, little need for specialized skills – is only going to attract such a pool. So if this is the pool you're going after in retail because it is the most economically viable even with all the call-offs and no-shows, the retail industry must have determined that this is better than going after more seasoned workers who would treat the job more seriously but who you'd have to pay more.

Sears used to employ full-time people selling clothes, appliances, and other products. Then they decided that it made more economic sense to make people part-time. Why? One reason is because then you don't have to offer health insurance.

The United States is the only country in the developed world in which employers are burdened with having to provide health insurance to full-time employees. In all other developed countries, the government provides national health insurance to all citizens. Employers are not involved, nor are private insurers that have a fiduciary responsibility to maximize profits. This is why the United States pays more for health care than any other country and is the only developed country in which millions of people don't have health insurance.

Given the political divide in the United States, national health insurance is unlikely to happen anytime soon. It could be done most simply by expanding Medicare to cover all citizens rather than just those 65 and older. But this would deprive private insurers of huge profits, and the insurance lobby is a powerful force. It would also mean increased taxes, which almost no one wants, even if the increase would pale in comparison to what we currently pay in insurance premiums to for-profit insurers. Perhaps the biggest obstacle is that we're talking "socialized medicine," terminology that sends shivers down the spine of one of our political parties, even if it is how all other countries do it.

So, part-time people cost less because they don't get health insurance. The retailer has determined that the cost of the no-call, no-show is simply a necessary cost of doing business, like shoplifting. Rather than hire full-time store detectives to minimize theft, retailers have determined that would be more expensive than tolerating the level of theft they currently tolerate. The attendance issue is the same thing. Retailers have determined that high school part-timers can do this job. Even if they don't show up, thus increasing the workloads of their fellow employees and the store manager (who is also underpaid, by the way) to pick up the slack, it makes more economic sense to the retailer than hiring people who would take the job more seriously but also cost more.

That's pretty much it, folks. So it appears the no-call, no-show is also here to stay, at least until technology eliminates all of these jobs completely.

CHAPTER

13

Tis the Season

"It's the most wonderful time of the year ..."

This line from the popular Christmas song is about the joys of Christmas season. But for many retailers, it could also be about back-to-school season. And for some, 2021 was a banner year, with millions of students returning to the classroom after a long pandemic-induced hiatus.

According to Don Unser, chief retail strategist with the NPD Group Inc., spending on traditional back-to-school items soared much earlier in the year than usual in 2021. By early March, sales of backpacks, shoes and apparel had already surpassed 2020 full-year levels. During the last three weeks in April, "sales in these categories grew by triple digits versus 2020."

Phillip Jackson is chief commerce officer at Rightpoint Consulting, an IT service management company, and host of two popular podcasts, *Future Commerce* and *Merchant to Merchant*. He had predicted such an increase in back-to-school sales in 2021 due to pent-up demand created by the pandemic.

"After 18 months of remote learning, they'll need suitable clothes," he said. "They'll hit the stores for school clothes, uniforms, supplies and electronics."

Jackson said that while families spent a lot on pajamas during the pandemic, "spending on pants and tops declined. Unless their children didn't grow much over the past 18 months, families will need to purchase whole new school wardrobes for them." As for high schoolers and college students, "they may still fit into last year's clothes, but styles are changing. Skinny jeans are out, and wider, more relaxed cuts are in."

As for electronics, "most kids will need a device when they return to the classroom, as COVID-19 inserted a huge digital component to learning, including digital class schedules, syllabuses and learning materials," Jackson said.

While some schools provided devices free of charge to students during the pandemic, most school districts adopted "a BYOD policy" in 2021, "meaning parents will have to pay for a new device themselves" as well as reimburse the school if their child damaged or cannot return the school-issued device.

But Jackson also cautioned retailers not to get too jubilant over their prospective good fortune. "For parents, many of whom lost jobs or hours as a result of the pandemic, back-to-school will be more costly than ever."

While lucrative for retailers, back-to-school can also be a headache.

"In the shoe world, back to school is the money maker," says a shoe store manager in the Midwest. "Bigger than Christmas. Everyone needs new school shoes, new gym shoes, a book bag."

The downside for the shoe store employee is that nobody is allowed to take vacation during back-to-school season. Another downside is that the kids generally have to come in with their parents to buy their shoes.

"You might have a family of four all trying on shoes, throwing them on the floor, littering the aisles, fighting with each other. If you don't have their size, look out. You have screaming kids, angry moms. Everybody's looking for a deal."

Clothing purchases also create chaos at back-to-school time, again due largely to all the different sizes that must be in stock to make all the moms happy. Parents waiting till the last minute to buy their kids' school supplies are also a problem.

"The day before school starts is when many parents decide to do it, it seems," says one store employee. "Then, even a week later, you have people returning things because the school didn't allow black-soled gym shoes or something. So even a week later you're still dealing with back-to-school shoppers."

Until recently, stores like Target, Walmart and other department stores might get a master list of the school supplies needed from the local schools so they know how many No.2 pencils, spiral notebooks, etc., to stock up on. But they didn't get each child's specific classroom list of supplies.

"Customers would come in and ask what Joey needs for Mrs. Craft's third-grade class, like we were supposed to know," says one employee.

Now, some large retailers have online access to individual classroom supply requirements. But this is a very recent development.

For most retailers, the winter holidays still represent their most lucrative time. It used to be retailers would feast on Black Friday. The day after Thanksgiving was viewed by everyone as the official start of the Christmas season. While the origins of the name Black Friday vary depending on where you look, for retailers it signaled the time of year their profits moved from red to black.

Today, many Americans no longer participate in traditional Black Friday in favor of its online counterpart, Cyber Monday. In 2020, for the first time, more than half of American consumers did most or all of their Christmas shopping online. Of course, 2020 was not a typical year. Still, this trend was already in place.

Holiday season is different now than it used to be. In addition to Cyber Monday and all the online shopping people do, some stores now start their sales before Thanksgiving. In recent years, many large retailers broke with tradition and were open on Thanksgiving. There are still people who will camp out for Black Friday and trip over each other to be the first ones in the store to get that great deal on a big screen TV – and then realize it won't fit in their car and they have no way to get it home – but there is no question the day has lost some of its luster.

Back when Black Friday was more of a thing, a mall might open at 5 in the morning to let in people who would then wait in line at the various stores that had special deals. In recent years many stores began opening at midnight the night before.

"Certain stores would have a bigger line than others," says one mall employee. "Victoria's Secret always had a giant line. I don't know what they were giving away."

Usually, sales were a little softer the few days leading up to Black Friday as retailers geared up for the onslaught.

"People would yell and scream about how they had waited in line all day when an item was not in stock in their size," says one retailer. "Then there were people wanting to return stuff that day and want the Black Friday price for something they bought two weeks ago."

In 2021, many large retailers like Target, Walmart and Best Buy changed their minds and decided to go back to being closed on Thanksgiving. The reasons they stated were gobbledygook. I believe it is due to the growing popularity of online versus in-person shopping combined with the backlash they may have received from making their employees work on Thanksgiving. Either way, it is unlikely that Black Friday will ever be the event it used to be. And I believe that's a good thing.

As for Christmas, there will always be the customers that accuse you of ruining their child's holiday because they waited until the last minute to get that year's hot toy and now it's not in stock. I am not one of those people but I can relate.

When the movie *Toy Story* came out, my son wanted the Buzz Lightyear action figure for Christmas. This was before virtually every product known to Man could be found online. I must have called or visited every toy store in the Chicago metropolitan area. No one had this thing.

My son had to do without it for Christmas that year. A few months later while on vacation in Florida I saw one at a Walmart and got it for him. I think they made a movie based on my experience called *Jingle All the Way* starring Arnold Schwarzenegger.

Christmas music played in stores during the Christmas season is a tradition that goes back as far as any of us can remember. Christmas music at Christmas time in a downtown Marshall Field's or Macy's generated a warm, nostalgic feeling.

Today, of course, even playing Christmas music at Christmas time has become controversial. Danny Turner, global senior vice president of programming for Mood Media, says retailers should carefully consider what music they play during what he calls "this era of hyper-sensitivity."

"A perfect example of this is the polarizing classic, *Baby it's Cold Outside,*" Turner says. "Widely revered as a holiday mainstay for decades, the classic tune was looked at through an entirely different lens last holiday season – a very appropriate new take and perspective given the sensitivities we've come to embrace in the #MeToo era."

I had never thought of that song as polarizing. In fact, it is probably my favorite of all the classic Christmas tunes (depending on who's singing it, of course). The lyrics do depict a man being persistent in trying to get a woman to stay the night over her objections, and I realize this is a behavior we need to temper in our society. But am I a sexist pig for feeling that it's just a song? Man's pursuit of Woman is as old as the hills. Particularly given the time period in which the song was written, it sounds to me more like innocent flirtation.

"As our social mores evolve and are less rooted in the common experience from the idyllic Christmas days of the 40s and 50s, patrons' expectations and willingness to accept holiday classics are changing," Turner says. "One bad customer experience can turn shoppers off to a brand."

He is referring to a customer bad-mouthing a company over social media, leading to "brand backlash." He says a customer offended by hearing *Baby it's Cold Outside* played in a store could lead them to "take to Instagram to leave rants in real time, and customer outrage can go viral in seconds."

Wow! Are that many people offended by that song? Perhaps my favorite rendition is sung by Zoe Deschanel in the movie *Elf* with Will Farrell. *Elf!*

Turner advises retailers to err on the side of caution, which means fewer retailers taking the risk of playing *Baby it's Cold Outside* in their stores. I guess it's a small price to pay for the safer and more enlightened society that will undoubtedly result. More important, it will keep retailers from having to suffer the wrath of offended customers.

"If your song selection makes just one of your brand loyalists feel uncomfortable, you've failed them," Turner says. "The holidays aren't a time to take a chance and push boundaries. What you don't play can't hurt you."

He has a point there. I cannot imagine customers complaining because a store is *not* playing *Baby it's Cold Outside*. How would they even know unless they were in the store for hours and never heard it?

But don't worry. If you like the tune, artists can always change the lyrics to bring it up to current moral standards. Maybe now the guy is trying to get the woman to leave but she doesn't want to because it's snowing. Now he's the jerk, trying to throw her out. Merry Christmas.

——— **CHAPTER** ———
14

Would you get the hell out of here already?

When I was a shipping clerk/stock boy at Best & Co. in high school, one of my duties was to stay until closing to lock up with the store manager. Best & Co. was a women's clothing store, and the store managers were all women. My friend Joel, with whom I shared the shipping clerk/stock boy job, and I were the only male employees (except for the shoe department, which was separate from Best & Co. and rented its space). Thus, it was for safety reasons that Joel or I stayed so the store manager on duty would not have to lock up alone.

The store closed at 9 p.m. during the week and 5:30 p.m. on Saturdays, but some shoppers seemed oblivious and continued shopping past those times. The store manager would go around and tell them the store was closed and gently request they finish up their shopping so we could go home. Many customers seemed indignant that the store had the nerve to close before they were ready.

"Christmas Eve in the mid-1980s I was working at a Kinney Shoes inside a mall in Racine, Wisconsin," says one store manager. "We lowered the metal gate at closing time to dissuade new customers from coming in while attempting to clear out the customers already in the store. People were crawling under the gate to get in. I told them we were closed.

I reminded them it was Christmas Eve. Crawling under the gate? Really? I told them my staff wants to go home."

A Target employee tells of a woman who always came in right before closing to get coffee and sit at the Starbucks that was in the store. "She would just sit there and get irate when anyone mentioned the store was closing. She would purposely take her time and not leave until she was made to leave. Then she wouldn't leave the parking lot, which had to be cleared before we could leave."

Another retail employee says "it's often people on drugs trying to steal that are still in the store 20 minutes after we close. They need money for drugs and think it might be easier to steal at night when there is less staff, especially at closing time when employees are focused on leaving. And they're right."

Then there are the people who, after the doors have been locked, come banging on the door pleading to be let in. "I just need one thing," they say. "I'll be really quick." There seem to be countless instances of this each day in the retail world.

"Whether it's procrastinators, last-minute shoppers, Christmas Eve, or the night before somebody's birthday, there is always someone who has some kind of buying emergency and has to do it right at closing time," one manager says.

Big department stores usually have intercoms over which they can announce the store is closing. If the intercom is not working, however, chaos can ensue.

"Our intercom was down for months," says one store manager. "So we no longer could make an announcement that 'the store will be closing in 30 minutes' or whatever. We had to go around and tell people."

She describes one incident in which a customer got indignant over the store having the audacity to close before she was done shopping.

"As usual, the store is full of people right before closing. There is a guest with a fairly full cart. At this point the store is now closed so we told the guest the store was closed and that she should start heading to the front. Well, the guest got indignant. She said, 'Well, I still need a few things.' She proceeds to shop and what could we do besides ask and ask and ask? But just very indignant like, how dare you tell me when I'm done shopping?"

You would think such issues would not arise at much smaller stores but apparently this is not the case. The manager of a small shoe store in a suburban mall relates the following incident.

"It was closing time. We had a gate, so we put the gate down. There were still a couple people in the store but we would put the gate down, then raise it to let them out. This woman comes by who earlier in the evening had put some shoes on hold. We always tell people that we will hold them until the end of the night. Normally we would not let someone in once the gate is down. But since there were still a couple people checking out and this customer had the item on hold, we opened the gate and let her in.

"First, she insists on trying on the shoes again. Then she wants to use an expired coupon. Then her credit card is declined. Then she wants to call her bank to see why her card was declined. All in all, we were in the store at least an extra 30 minutes. And then, of course, she didn't even buy the shoes because she didn't have any money."

On that note, I would like to start bringing this narrative to a close. I hope you learned something. I know I learned a lot while working on it. I learned so much I think I could manage my own store. I would manage it much differently than most other stores are managed. The final chapter describes how I would manage my own store, if I had one.

My Store

CHAPTER

15

How I would do things

So many things I would do differently if I had my own store. I don't know what kind of store it would be exactly. I'm picturing something larger than a shop in a mall but smaller than a Walmart. I don't know what I would sell; a variety of merchandise, let's say. It's a hypothetical store so it really doesn't matter.

At my store, the hiring process would be me talking to a person for 10 minutes to decide if they are mature, smart, honest, and of high character. I have always prided myself on being a good judge of character, and character is what I would look for. I would offer more money than you'd make at other retail establishments, but I would only hire people who would take the job seriously.

I guess if I'm hiring mostly full-time people, I would have to offer health insurance. While I am against this burden that only this country imposes on private employers, I know I must do this if I want good people. The only other alternative would be to pay them enough to afford their own health insurance.

Attendance would not be an issue because of the kind of people I'd hire but the policy would be this: To miss work you must be seriously ill or have a genuine emergency. If I think your reason is bullshit or this happens more than once, I'll get someone else. In 50 years of working, I can count

77

on one hand the times I missed work for any reason. Go ahead and sue me. The only thing employers need worry about is discrimination and I would not discriminate. Regardless of race, religion, or sexual orientation, if you can't show up every day, you're gone.

Obviously, if you steal from me, you're gone. But again, I would not hire people who would steal or miss work in the first place unless I misjudged their character.

At my store, employees would be called "employees." The word "employee" is not derogatory. People roll their eyes at companies that think calling employees associates, team members, cast members or crew members will make them feel better about themselves or make the company seem more democratic. My employees would not care what they were called as long as they're paid well and treated with respect.

Similarly, at my store we would call customers "customers," not guests, clients, or anything else. In my store, they are not guests. I did not invite these people. They come of their own volition to buy something. We would not be rude to customers because without them we'd have no business. We would be extremely courteous and helpful if our customers needed help with anything. But the relationship is purely transactional.

I would not invest in "facial recognition" technology for any reason, although I'd probably have security cameras. I would not invest in technology to go "cashless" or "cashier-less" either. No self-service kiosks. If I had a McDonald's, the "guest experience leader" would be behind the counter or in the kitchen making burgers rather than forcing people to use fecal-contaminated touch screens.

If my store had checkout aisles, one would not be self-checkout. I don't want the headaches, nor do I want to pay someone to supervise the self-checkout. I'd rather pay an efficient, dedicated cashier. I don't want artificial intelligence. I'd rather have actual intelligence. She would also be fast, pleasant, and motivated.

I use the pronoun "she" because most if not all of my cashiers would be female. I think women are generally nicer than men and I want that kind of personality at the checkout. I wouldn't officially limit the cashier position to women. That would be discriminatory. I'm just telling you this. And I find men who are too nice to be a little creepy. Call me what you will. This is my store.

If I employ baggers, speed and efficiency are important there too. I find the personal interaction between bagger and customer to be less intimate than that between cashier and customer, so I might employ men as well as women as baggers. I don't want to look like I only hire women, although my gut finds women preferable to men for most customer-facing jobs.

Whether male or female, cashier or bagger, at my store I'd hire people who can scan and bag items fast. When I'm in a line and the people ringing me up and bagging my stuff do it at an agonizingly slow pace, I am frustrated not just by how long they're taking, but by the question: Why did the store hire this person to work checkout? A lot of these people are elderly. Who thinks this is a good idea?

I'm all for equal opportunity. Okay, I can understand why you might question this given my opinions on gender roles above. But I really do support hiring older people for some jobs. Just not this one. And while I realize bagging groceries is not difficult and thus almost anyone can do it, it seems that speed should be a primary job requirement. The elderly do not come to mind as ideal candidates.

At my store, if we have a breakroom, there will be no goodies brought in for people's birthdays, work anniversaries or other events. It's not that I am a curmudgeon, even though I am. I just don't need the wasted time and energy.

For example, one day at my wife's Target, the team leads were supposed to bring in goodies for the staff. "The problem is, if we put them all out in the morning, the people who work later won't get any," my wife fretted. Her solution: "Divide them into three portions and label them morning, afternoon and evening."

At my store, this situation would never arise because, number one, I wouldn't care who got goodies and who didn't, but more importantly, I would nip the potential problem in the bud by prohibiting goodies in the first place. Baking them, bringing them in and worrying about who gets what are activities that do not in any way help my business. And the employees I'd hire wouldn't care.

At my store, we would not honor expired coupons or competitor's coupons. There'd be no price match if a product is cheaper somewhere else. I'm not going to apologize, get defensive, or fear losing your business. I'd encourage you to buy the product elsewhere if you could get it cheaper there.

At my store, if employees see someone stealing, they can confront them, embarrass them, call the cops, and I'd support them every step of the way. In fact, thwarting theft would be one of their main job responsibilities. The employees wandering the aisles would double as full-time security guards and would be authorized to be as rude as they need to be to keep you from walking off with shit that I paid for like it's some God-given right. Not at my store. All I'd ask my employees is to be sure. I'll have enough lawsuits on my hands.

It's not just shoplifters I'd authorize my employees to confront. Any "Karen" making any over-the-top demand or behaving rudely can also be asked to leave. If they threaten to never shop at the store again, we'd thank them. If they're a pain in the ass, I don't want their business. Any customer that throws something at me or one of my staff gets charged with assault.

If your kids act up in the store, you could be asked to leave. Any teens making trouble with no intent to buy will be asked to leave and threatened with trespassing charges or worse. "You can't do that. We have rights," they'll say as I dial up the police and report a group of teens that won't leave the store.

I don't think I'd offer online ordering, curbside pickup, or delivery. We're a small store. I don't want to deal with it. I'm certainly not partnering with Amazon, Apple, Google or whomever so people can sit on their asses eating out of Styrofoam containers watching "The Bachelor" and say, "Siri, I want a pack of Juicy Fruit," and I have to get the pack of gum delivered. You want something from my store, you come in and buy it and take it home with you.

In real life, I might go out of business. But this is hypothetical. And it's my store.

No returns without a receipt. If a product has been opened or used, no return unless the product is defective. If you have a receipt for a product that has not been opened or used and return it within 30 days, I'll take it back and give you a full refund – on your debit or credit card if that is what you used to buy the product, or in cash if you paid cash. No merch credits. No exceptions. Not complicated.

I don't know if I'd sell gift cards. But I'm not going to go out of my way to educate people to keep them from getting scammed. I don't think that's my responsibility.

My wife told me Target was giving all its hourly employees another $200 bonus in 2021 and that a lot of them complained that taxes would be taken out so they wouldn't get the full $200. First, my employees would understand that all income is taxed and wouldn't be so unappreciative. However, if I were giving them all $200 bonuses, I'd give them each two crisp $100 bills and pick up the tax.

Target, Walmart, Taco Bell, Disney, and other companies have also enhanced their education assistance programs to attract employees in a tight job market. In July 2021, Walmart announced it will pay the full cost of tuition and books at select institutions for its 1.5 million part-time and full-time Walmart and Sam's Club workers. Target followed with plans to spend $200 million over the next four years on educational benefits for its U.S. full- and part-time employees.

While I think free tuition is great, I would not offer such a benefit at my store. If my employees want to pursue a degree or some sort of academic or vocational training so they no longer have to work for me, that is their business, as long as it doesn't interfere with their job. But I would not spend my money to fund these ambitions. I'd take that $200 million and pay them more. Then if they want to use it to further their education, so be it.

We'd be closed Thanksgiving and Christmas, open 7 a.m. to 9 p.m. all other days. At 9 p.m., the registers lock up (not really but this is what we'd tell customers) so if you want to buy something you better do it by then. Anyone still in the store at 9 will be ushered out. When they become indignant and vow never to shop at the store again, I'll simply tell them that if I could have closed at 6, I would have.

In fact, working retail is a nightmare. I'd probably sell my store before I'd make a lifetime of it. Any buyers out there? The world is nuts, so there must be. And thank you from the bottom of my heart for reading this book.